Finding Your Own Eden

There's a Place for You in the Pacific Northwest

John Hanna

Seattle, Washington
Portland, Oregon
Denver, Colorado
Vancouver, B.C.
Scottsdale, Arizona

Copyright © 1997 John R. Hanna
All rights reserved. No part of this publication may be reproduced without express written permission of the publisher, except in the case of brief quotations embodied in critical articles or reviews.

ISBN# 0-89716-755-4
LOC# 97-68357
01.0107
Cover photos: Wayne Shuman
Cover design: David Marty
Editing & Production: Elizabeth Lake

First printing October 1997
10 9 8 7 6 5 4 3 2 1

Peanut Butter Publishing
Pier 55, Ste. 301 1101 Alaskan Way • Seattle, WA 98109-2982
(206) 748-0345 • FAX (206) 748-0343
Portland, OR (503) 222-5527 • Denver, CO (303) 322-0065
Vancouver, B.C. (604) 688-0320 • Scottsdale, AZ (602) 947-3575
e mail: pnutpub@aol.com
WWW home page: http://www.pbpublishing.com

Printed in Canada

Dedication

This book is dedicated to Gregoriann, my wife. Her encouragement, patience and sharp eye made this book possible!

Table of Contents

Acknowledgments 9

Introduction 11

United States 17
    WASHINGTON 19
        Washington Coast 22
            Long Beach Peninsula 23
            Aberdeen-Hoquim-Cosmopolis 25
            Ocean Shores 27
        Kitsap Peninsula 29
            Port Orchard 31
            Silverdale 34
            Poulsbo 35
        Olympic Peninsula 37
            Port Ludlow 38
            Port Townsend 39
            Sequim 42
            Port Angeles 45

        Northwestern Washington 47
            Anacortes 49
            Bellingham 52

        North Central Washington 55
            Leavenworth 57
            Chelan 59
            Wenatchee 62
        Okanogan County - Omak and Okanogan ... 65

        Northeastern Washington 68
            Colville 69

        Southeastern Washington 72
            Walla Walla, College Place,
            and Milton Freewater, Oregon 73

- OREGON 77
  - Oregon Coast 78
    - Astoria 81
    - Newport 83
    - Florence 86
    - Coos Bay 87
    - Brookings 89
  - Willamette Valley 91
    - Silverton 92
    - Corvallis 94
    - Eugene 96
  - Umpqua and Rogue Valleys 100
    - Roseburg 100
    - Grants Pass 102
    - Medford 105
    - Ashland 108
  - Central Oregon 110
    - Hood River 113
    - Redmond 115
    - Sisters 117
    - Bend 119
    - Klamath Falls 122
  - Northeastern Oregon 124
    - Enterprise 126
    - La Grande 129
    - Baker City 131

- IDAHO 135
  - Panhandle 137
    - Bonners Ferry 138
    - Sandpoint 140
    - Coeur d'Alene 143
  - Central Idaho 146
    - Lewiston and Clarkston 147
    - McCall 150

Southern Idaho	153
Boise	154
Ketchum, Sun Valley and Elkhorn	157
Stanley	159
Salmon	161
MONTANA	**165**
Kalispell	167
Whitefish	171
Missoula	173
Hamilton	175
Butte	178
Bozeman	181
Helena	184
Canada	**187**
BRITISH COLUMBIA	189
Penticton	194
Kelowna	198
Kamloops	201
Whistler	203
Victoria	207
Nanaimo	211
Some Advice	215
Order Form	219

Acknowledgments

My thanks goes to all of the Chamber of Commerce, real estate and business people who took their time to talk with me and provide me with the information about their communities. I would have liked to include all their names but that would fill up several pages and economy of time and materials would not allow it. I apologize for not being able to mention them individually.

There are those that are close to this project that deserve special recognition. Wayne Shuman was my companion for most of the trips and helped immensely with the first editing. Wayne is also responsible for the cover photos. David Marty designed the cover and did a great job. John Betrozoff and Rich Skinner read the first draft and offered a number of valuable suggestions. Mike Pastore, an experienced author, offered some great advice and kept encouraging me—Thanks Mike! Of course my wife edited and encouraged me and for that I am deeply grateful. Then there are the countless friends who kept reminding me that I was writing a book and they wanted to know how it was coming. I don't know if they know it but their encouragement meant a lot to me.

The final editing was a great help in producing a book that was professionally done. For that help I am indebted to Liz Lake, a thoughtful and fine professional.

To write a book is one thing but to have others use it requires someone who knows how to get it printed. For that task I turned to Elliott Wolf who led me through the publishing maze with skill and sensitivity. Bernie Ornelas guided the marketing of this book and gave me a great many valuable suggestions.

To all those mentioned above a great big thanks!

Introduction

Many city dwellers long for a life that is less stressful and closer to what they envision as idyllic. They are looking for a place where the air is fresh and the water is pure; where they know their neighbors and where giving and receiving a helping hand is not a novelty. They want a place where the children or grandchildren can safely go to the "ol' swimmin' hole", stop on the way home to contemplate the sails of the great ships that float across the beautiful blue skies; a place where the child and the adult can come to know the wonderful feeling of contentment that comes from reading a good book, in front of a crackling fire, on a peaceful snowy day.

It is obvious to me, after listening to my friends, reading the newspapers and watching TV, that urban life is taking it's toll. The urban dweller is confronted with constant aggravations brought on by population increase with its attendant problems such as smog, pollution, crime and violence, crowded freeways, zoning restrictions, growth management and on and on.

It is no wonder that rural areas are experiencing a resurgence. For example, it was reported in 1996, in a local Seattle newspaper, that in the early 1990s, the population of Washington's rural areas grew by 100,000. I think I wouldn't be too far from wrong if I guessed there is another 100,000 people just waiting for the chance to bolt and run to join their fellow urbanites in the "country."

For any number of years urban dwellers have longed for a simpler life but the job would not allow relocation. This restriction, for many, has disappeared today because of the advances in technology. Society has reach a point where, because of the sophistication of communication and transportation systems, it is possible for some to live considerable distant from the employment source.

Reported in the *Seattle Times* in April of 1997 is the story of Boeing joining with Microsoft and Teledesic in a gigantic effort to establish a system of 300 communication satellites. These vessels will encircle the globe and make com-

Introduction

munications from "the smallest villages to the business centers worldwide" a common occurrence. Just think about the impact this will have on business and industry. People will be able to locate any place on earth and still be in the "mainstream" of things.

At present the software designer, the consultant, the network marketer, the specialist, the writer, the industrialist, the lecturer, only needs a phone line, a fax, a computer and a modem to communicate with the client or headquarters. Video phone conferencing has progressed to the point that it is commonplace in business and industry. It is even available for home use and the prices are reasonable. There are others who can take advantage of the advances in communication and transportation technology to locate where they want. Take for example the commercial pilot, who with the present efficiencies in air travel, can be at his job part of the week on the Los Angeles to Tokyo flight and then take the rest of the week to tend a ranch in Idaho. What about the sales representative whose territory is the Pacific Northwest? Perhaps Coeur d'Alene, with nearby Spokane and its national and international airport, is a better home location for him and his family than Seattle. What difference does it make if a patent attorney lives near Boise or Portland while his client lives in Malaysia? The phone and computer communications quality will be much the same.

With today's communication and transportation systems, it really doesn't make much difference where people are located. Imagine what it will be like when the satellite system is in the air in a few short years and Boeing or Airbus comes up with a new model of supersonic jet that will carry hundreds of passengers at speeds and distances now hard to imagine.

The above has to do with the impact the technological world is having on business and industry. A paradigm shift brought on by technology is leading business and industry to discover that it is no longer necessary for people to be tied to a work station in a central location. With the event of computers, faxes and satellites, plus advances in transportation, it is now possible to have an organization, once restricted to a

Introduction

building(s) in a given location, that stretches over the nation or even the world.

Another group that has the freedom to locate where they choose are the retired. Many of these folks are looking for a place where they can slow down a bit and enjoy some of the finer and simpler things of life. A place where the pension might be stretched, where that long delayed garden can be planted, where they can raise some chickens or lambs. Perhaps they just want a place where they can sit on the front porch, with a glass of lemonade and watch the sun sink away from their favorite place on this "good" earth.

One also has to be realistic when considering relocations. There are those city dwellers who must live near where they work. But they do go on vacations and many dream of a vacation cabin on a beautiful little lake or in a peaceful mountain valley. A place where the fishing is good, a garden will thrive, the water is clear and the people friendly. One only has to visit the Sisters area in Oregon to know of such a place. There one soon becomes enchanted by the blue skies, the snowcapped Cascades and the sweet scent of the Ponderosa. Visualize for a moment a cozy warm cabin nestled in among the pines, with "ol Shep" standing guard on the front porch while the family gathers around the roaring fireplace to hear grandpa and grandma tell about the "old days". What a treat that would be for a family!

What is wrong with a young family finding such a place? A place they can buy and build a small cabin that can be used for vacations while the family is growing. A place, when the time comes, that will serve as their retirement nest.

My wife and I spent two years scouting for an area where we wanted to retire. Before starting the search we sat down and developed a criteria to guide our search. First, we decided that our retirement home should not be more than two hours from the city. We wanted a view, waterfront would be nice but not essential. Other homes should be located near by for security. Also, we wanted utilities readily available and a price within our means.

After many miles, and countless possibilities, we finally found our property. It was one hour from the city, on an island with the building site on a cliff overlooking a beautiful

Introduction

waterway called Saratoga Passage—a part of Puget Sound It has a view of the Olympic Mountains and Whidbey Island. A tram takes its passengers down 250 feet to a nice beach. Great neighbors are nearby. The utilities are located on the site. The price was within our means and as an added bonus—the lot's value has doubled.

After this experience, I started thinking that not everybody has the time to conduct a two year search for their place. It occur to me that others might profit from my experience. It was at this time that I decided to write this book to help others identify communities that might appeal to them for retirement or relocation purposes.

My task became one of identifying a number of communities in the beautiful Pacific Northwest that might fit the criteria of those who are looking for their "dream" home. Most of the communities in the book are small, rural in nature but large enough that they provide most of the essential services to which many urban dwellers are accustomed. The majority of the smaller communities are less than two hours away from the medical, business and retail services of a larger community.

Also described are some medium size communities. Medium size communities are helpful in avoiding the "cultural shock" some urban dwellers might experience in the process of community "downsizing".

The book does not describe the greater Seattle/Tacoma area, Spokane, Portland or Vancouver B.C. It is felt that these communities are familiar to most folks. They also have many of the qualities from which people are trying to escape. Don't get the wrong idea, I live in a suburb of Seattle and I am surviving quite well. There are many folks who really enjoy the excitement and challenge of a big city but there are those who don't—thus one of the reasons for this book.

In the body of the book, states and regions are described to give a person a larger view of the area in which specific communities are located. Descriptions of the communities include general descriptive information, economic drivers, real estate costs, community services such as police, fire protection, education, medical facilities, etc. Also included in the community descriptions is information on the cultural and rec-

Introduction

reational opportunities, climate, proximity and, finally, a summary.

It is suggested that the book be used as a reference. The state and regional descriptions are designed to give the reader a general view of the areas. The community descriptions provide more details regarding a particular community and the summary presents community highlights.

If a reader is not familiar with the states or regions, they might want to look at these sections first. Once they find a region that appeals to them, they might want to read the summaries of the communities in that region. If a summary appeals to them, then reading the community description will fill in some of the important details.

It is felt that the information is generally accurate and should remain so for a number of years. Drastic change in communities is rare unless there is some type of economic boon, downturn or a natural disaster.

How was the information collected for the book? First, the author, with input from a number of friends, selected 98 communities to contact. A letter introducing myself and the project, along with a request for information was sent to the selected communities' Chambers of Commerce. Eighty-five of the communities responded. The information from the 85 respondents was reviewed and 67 communities were visited. The visits were comprised of interviews with Chamber personnel (the manager or director), Realtors or economic development agency personnel. Sixty of the original 67 communities were finally included in the book. In addition to the visits, hundreds of brochures, pamphlets and resource materials were reviewed.

Please look upon a community as a "greater community". For example, when reviewing Eugene one should not limit themselves to the city limits but should also look at some of the smaller nearby communities, e.g., Coburg, Junction City, Cottage Grove. These might be more attractive to a person depending on what they have in mind for a home site. These communities are near enough to Eugene that a person can take advantage of the city and its amenities.

Why were some communities left out of the book. Some were left out because the author just plain ran out of time. My

Introduction

apologies to those communities—perhaps in a second edition. A number don't appear because they lacked appeal, were experiencing economic difficulties or lacked housing opportunities. Although obvious, it must be stated that the appeal of a community was simply my personal bias.

In closing, I would like to invite you to the Pacific Northwest. I've lived in the Southeast, Northeast, Midwest and in the Pacific Northwest. There are many beautiful place in North America but the Pacific Northwest has to be one of the grandest.

My hope is that this book will be helpful to you in your quest to find your Eden—remember, there's a place for you in the Pacific Northwest.

Sincerely,
John R. Hanna

United States

Washington Map

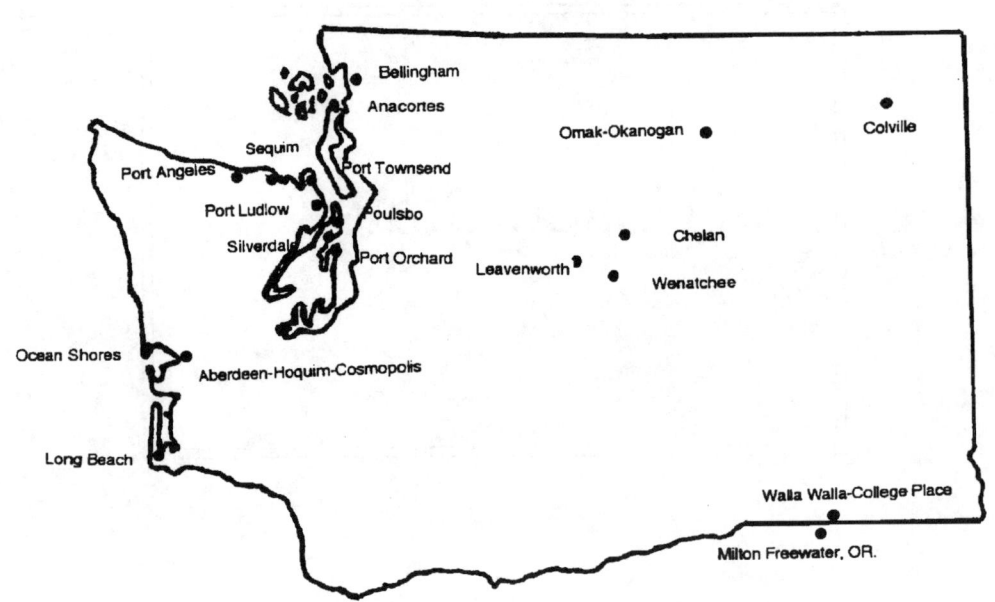

WASHINGTON
(Pop. 5,343,000)

For a person raised in Iowa and Kansas, Washington is about as near to paradise as one can find in this lifetime. It has the tall snow-capped mountains, green forest and a wonderful sea coast that everyone sees on the calendars or in *National Geographic*. This state, like other Northwestern states, is much more than beautiful scenery.

The state has what might be call a "dual personality". It is divided between the east and west by a spectacular range of mountains called the Cascades. These mountains have a great impact on the weather of the two parts. The mountains act as a barrier and the moisture supplied by the Pacific is dropped mostly on their western side. What moisture is left is then shared with the east side. This makes for an exciting contrast. The west side is characterized by its greenness and mild climate, while the east side is more likely to be brown, drier and have a climate that is more extreme.

There are some interesting facts about Washington. It has some rather high mountains for the continental United States. Mt. Rainier is 14, 410 feet with Mt. Adams at 12,307 and Mt. Baker is over 10,000 feet. The state, in square miles, is as big as all of New England. It has 3000 miles of coast line, 1000 lakes, and a great ocean inlet called Puget Sound. There are 26 Indian reservations in Washington, deserts, rain forests, fields of golden grains, apple orchards, great dams, countless islands, fields covered with tulips and daffodils, salmon and whales, giant airplanes, a vast ferry fleet, submarines and aircraft carriers, cougars, bears, great Roosevelt elk herds and some of the nicest people a person will ever meet.

Western Washington will get rainfalls that range from 200 inches in the Olympic Mountains' rain forest to as little as 13 inches in the "rain shadow" of those mountains. Most of Western Washington is blessed with an annual rainfall of 35 up to 60 inches in a few sections. Seattle, for example will get 35 inches, on the average, which compares with New York City and Chicago. Summer temperatures rarely get into the 90s. Normal temperatures in the summer run in the 70s and low 80s. Humidity is rarely a problem. Winters are mild with

Washington

temperatures ranging in the 30s and 40s. Snow fall, except in the mountains, is rarely bothersome. If it does snow, it is usually only around for a day or two. The weather, year around, in Western Washington is probably about as agreeable as one will find in the United States.

Eastern Washington is the place where the Western Washingtonians go to get sunshine. This part of the state gets more sun, more snow and less rain than the west side. The humidity is low and so the high temperatures in the summers are tolerable. In the winter it rarely gets subzero but it can get cold. Since it is so dry, the 7-15 inches annual rainfall is, in most of the region, very important. Land that use to be like much of the Great American Desert, is now, thanks to the irrigation provided by the dams along the Columbia and Snake, turning it into bountiful garden spots. The northeastern and the southeastern corners of the state are slightly wetter and greener than the rest of this eastern portion.

The foundation of the economy for Washington is based on agriculture, wood products, fishing, shipping, aircraft construction, ship building and repair, tourism, military installations, computer technology and associated businesses and industries. Washington's proximity to the Pacific Rim countries is extremely beneficial to its business environment. It should also be mentioned that the state tax burden in Washington, according to *Kiplinger's Personal Finance Magazine* - August 1995, pp. 58-59, is the 14th lowest in the nation.

Real estate is the highest in and around the larger cities, e.g., Seattle, Tacoma, Spokane, Vancouver, and Bellevue. Seattle, Bellevue and the surrounding communities have the highest priced properties in the state. In this area a new three bedroom/two bath home will range in cost from a low of $150,000 to $250,000.

The rest of the state has real estate prices that are relatively low when compared to the larger cities of the East and West coasts. A new three bedroom/two bath home can be found in the low $100,000s in most places outside the larger urban areas of the state.

The public schools in the whole state are good. Almost half of the state's budget goes toward providing education for

Washington

the state's young folks. There are over forty, 4 or 2 year, degree-granting institutions.

Health care in Washington is some of the finest in the nation. It is said that the Seattle area is one of the safest places in the world to have a heart attack. The response time is just short of miraculous. The world acclaimed Fred Hutchison Cancer Center is located in Seattle. The nationally acclaimed hospital and medical research center at the University of Washington is a leader in medical research. Washington State University is outstanding in the area of agriculture and veterinary medicine. There are a number of hospitals spread throughout the state that are capable of delivering comprehensive medical services. The smaller cities and towns also provides excellent medical services and are backup by the larger medical centers in nearby cities.

Culturally, the state is quite sophisticated. One will find splendid opportunities in the larger cities to enjoy opera, symphony, ballet, theater, museums, zoos, aquariums, the works of nationally recognized writers and artists, cinema productions and professional sports. Of course, smaller communities have their own unique cultural and entertainment opportunities and they also partake of the larger events taking place in the metropolitan regions.

Every type of recreational activity one can imagine is available. Some of the highlights are such things as downhill skiing at one of the 10 or so ski areas. There is cross country skiing, snowmobiling, ice fishing, deep sea fishing, crabbing, clamming, hunting, whitewater rafting, hiking, mountain climbing, biking, camping and boating. Washington is one of the boating meccas of the world. The excitement felt by an ardent boater upon seeing the thousands of boats in the Puget Sound area is something to behold. Seattle is just the tip of the iceberg when one considers boating in Washington. If one goes to Eastern Washington, it is amazing to see the number of boating opportunities available in this supposedly dry area. The dams on the Columbia and Snake Rivers make wonderful large lakes for boating. It is difficult to get used to going by a farm that is irrigating the dry land and see a 26 foot cabin cruiser parked next to the barn.

Washington

Washington Coast

Once a person crosses the Columbia River at Astoria, Oregon and heads north into Washington, the coast flattens and takes on many of the characteristics of the East coast of the United States. The sandy beaches are long and flat. Some of the longest beaches in the nation exist on this stretch of the coast.

The huge protected Willipa Bay, located on the southern portion of the coast, is an area where oysters, evergreen forests and wildlife abound. Further up the coast one comes to another large inlet called Grays Harbor. At the entrance to the harbor is the town of Westport, a destination sport fishing port. Across the harbor entrance is Ocean Shores, a popular retirement and resort community. At the eastern end of the harbor is Aberdeen, the largest community on the Washington coast.

Farther north the coast takes on a more rugged appearance. The Quinault Indian Reservation and the Olympic National Park come down to meet the Pacific. Highway 109 follows the coast line for about 24 miles and then ends at Taholah. The major road, Highway 101, generally does not follow the coast except for a small portion of about 15 miles. The lack of roads along this portion of the coast makes the shoreline less accessible to the general public. The northern part of the coast is very primitive and is a favorite hiking area. The northern tip of the Washington coast is capped by Cape Flattery and Tatoosh Island. These features signal the entrance to the Strait of Juan de Fuca.

Some of the wildlife one can see or find evidence of are Roosevelt elk, black bear, white tail deer, and cougar. In the ocean, gray whales, seals, dolphins and "Killer Whales" are present. Like all coasts, fishing is a major activity. The coast is on the migratory path of birds and consequently bird watching is matchless. There are a number of wildlife refuges along the coast. The forests consist of hemlock, Sitka spruce, Douglas fir, cedar, alder, maple and the everpresent shore pine.

Rain and storms are familiar visitors during the winter to the Washington coast. The summers are mild and the sun shines brightly during July, August and September.

Washington

The main industries are wood products, fishing, shell fish harvesting, tourism and agriculture. Like Oregon, the spotted owl controversy has had a negative impact on the wood products industry This has caused many of the coastal communities to look for diversification opportunities. Retraining of workers is a primary focus of many of the educational institutions. Commercial fishing is also experiencing a downturn. The quantity of fish has lessened. The problem appears to be associated with fishing moratoriums, dams, and poor fishing practices of the past.

The Washington Coast, except for the northern 1/3, is definitely different than the Oregon coast. Tourist traffic is less than one will find along many coasts in the West. This coast is a place to relax, think, read, walk, fly kites, fish, gather clams, eat oysters, drink coffee, play cards and talk to someone close to you about the finer things in life.

The areas selected for investigation were the Aberdeen/Hoquim/Cosmopolis area and Ocean Shores. Although not originally selected, the Long Beach area was visited as well. Let us start with the Long Beach area first.

Long Beach Peninsula

This Peninsula is a two mile wide, 28 mile long sandy flat arm of land. It forms the west side of Willipa Bay and provides protection to that body of water from the Pacific Ocean. The peninsula is primarily a resort area and consists of five very small communities, the largest being Long Beach (Pop. 1,236).

The beauty of the Peninsula is captured in its wonderful long beach, lakes, cranberry bogs, colorful rhododendrons and a great wildlife reserve. Driving down the spine of the peninsula one can not help but be struck by the similarity between this area and certain parts of the East coast.

The late spring, summers and fall are very pleasant and, during that period, the peninsula is crowded with sightseers and vacationers. It rains in the winter, just like the rest of the Pacific Northwest coast.

The economy is based on tourism and some production of cranberries and oysters. The downtowns have a number of shops and amusement facilities that cater to the visitors. The winters will still bring the visitors who want to get away from hectic urban life, enjoy an exciting Pacific storm or just read a good book and walk on the beach. The Peninsula is popular with retirees and they help to provide a good economic base.

The peninsula is a fine place for summer vacation homes. It can also provide a nice permanent residence for someone who is not tied to the urban areas for a living or is retired. Real estate prices are reasonable. Ocean front lots cost between $50,000 to $100,000. Ocean view lots can be purchased for $40,000 to $85,000. A good existing home can be purchased for $130,000 to $300,000. Properties on the Willipa Bay side of the peninsula appear to be less expensive than on the ocean beach side. If a person visits the peninsula he should drop by the village of Oysterville located at the northern end of the peninsula - its a gem. It's homes and church date from the late 1800s.

There are a number of things to do on the Peninsula. Bird watching, people watching during the summer, fishing, kite flying, horseback riding, boating and partaking of the entertainment are all available for the tourist. Long Beach is famous for its Washington State International Kite Festival, jazz festivals and a splendid annual car show.

This peninsula is 110 miles from Portland and 180 miles from the Seattle area. Portland, the closest urban center, is important to many areas in southwestern Washington for its shopping, advanced medical care, professional sports, cultural and entertainment activities and the excitement afforded by a large urban center.

Summary: Long Beach has a resort atmosphere. In the warm months it is busy and crowded with visitors. In the cooler months it has a much slower pace. It is a beautiful place and, with the Pacific Ocean right next door, the weather can be either very calm and relaxing or quite exciting. Real estate prices are quite reasonable by West coast standard. The area is somewhat isolated from the larger urban areas. Winters can be long and gray but a wonderful time for restoration of one's body and soul. The delightful summers usually make up for the winters. There is something about this area that promotes a feeling of nostalgia and thoughts about how life was really meant to be lived.

Aberdeen-Hoquim-Cosmopolis (26,500 Pop.)
(For clarity purposes this tri-city community will be referred to simply as Aberdeen -16,600 Pop.)

Aberdeen is the only coastal deep-water port north of San Francisco. This city is at the eastern terminus of Grays Harbor and is at the southern end of the Olympic Peninsula. The surrounding area is complete with green forests, long flat beaches, beautiful farms and views of the gorgeous Olympic mountains.

G. Scott Thomas ranked Aberdeen, in his recent book, *Rating Guide to Life in America's Small Cities*, 10th out of 219 cities. The ranking was based on information from the 1990 U.S. Census. The categories he used for the rating were recreational opportunities, economics, education, health care, public safety, transportation, proximity to urban areas and sophistication.

The economy of the area is supported by wood products, agriculture, commercial fishing, port services, boat building and tourism. Eighty-eight percent of the land base in this area is renewable forest. The downturn in logging has had a serious impact on this Washington community. A retraining program is being strongly pursued by the community. The Grays Harbor Community College is playing an important part in the retraining program. Diversity has become the focus of the business interests in Aberdeen. One of the results of this focus is the new state prison being built there. The Grays Harbor port is well positioned for shipping to and from the Pacific Rim countries. The port and community are at the western terminus of a major railroad. Grays Harbor is the largest exporter of logs of any port in the United States.

A unique feature of this tri-city area is a 4 lane highway connecting it with the urban centers to the east. Highway 12 is the only 4 lane road in Washington and Oregon that goes from the interior to the coast. This is economically beneficial to the community and especially the port.

Washington

Affordable housing is available. Remember, this area has always been a "mill town". As such, many of the areas near the rivers are made up of small, older houses. When housing is being discussed here, the focus will be on the homes in the hills surrounding the towns. Of course, if one is into rehabilitation, these small homes present a good business opportunity.

An older, three bedroom/two bath home with a view can cost in the low $100,000 range. Newer homes, similar in size, will cost in the mid $100,000s. Large homes with view and some vintage architecture will go as high as the $300,000s.

Aberdeen has a 259 bed hospital, Grays Harbor Community Hospital, which provides for regional medical care. There are over 100 health care providers in the community. The area has a 911 system.

Police and fire departments are staffed with full-time officers. The police staffing ratio is better than most small cities in the United States.

The Grays Harbor Community College serves the community and has an excellent retraining program. The public schools are good.

The climate is mild, with winter temperatures averaging a high of 48 degrees and a low of 36 degrees. The summers are also mild with an average high temperature of 72 degrees and a low of 50 degrees. Precipitation (56-84 inches annually) is greatest in the winter (78%). The summers are much drier. In case there is any doubt, the climate is definitely marine. The air of the area has been called some of most pristine in the country.

In Hoquim a person will see evidence of the rich past. The Hoquim Castle, built by the lumber baron Robert Lytle in 1897, is open for tours in the summer. This splendid example of homes of the past sports a 600 piece crystal chandelier, rosewood piano and other fine furnishings of the time.

The cultural activities are plentiful. Theater is well represented with the Driftwood Players, the Grayland Players and the Historical Seventh Street Theater. The Grays Harbor Art League sponsors local art shows. There is a civic choir and a symphony orchestra. A Dixieland Jazz Festival is a highlight

Washington

in February. For the outdoor person there is great hunting, fishing, boating, hiking and bird watching.

This tri-city area is in close proximity to urban areas. Seattle is 109 miles away, Olympia is 49 miles east and Portland is 140 miles to the southeast.

Summary: This is an area looking for new businesses. The retraining programs are producing a skilled work force. The new prison will bring a number of jobs, both with the construction and operation. The public services are good and the cultural and recreational opportunities are numerous. Real estate is quite reasonable. If one feels the positive features of the community are a fair trade-off for the rainy and gray winters, then the Aberdeen area is worth a serious look.

Ocean Shores (2,800 Pop.)

Ocean Shores is located on a long narrow, 6,000 acre peninsula at the mouth of Grays Harbor. It is a relatively young community, getting its start as a resort/retirement destination in the 1960s. This community is blessed with a lovely long beach just made for strolling and kite flying. The community supports an 18 hole PGA golf course. Ocean Shores, because of its flatness, is a grand place for biking. Relaxation and peace seem to exemplify life in Ocean Shores.

The community is a place for families and fun. There are ample grocery stores, pharmacies, clothing and sporting goods stores. What is not in Ocean Shores can be found in Aberdeen, 23 miles to the east. The tourist/convention business is the largest enterprise in the community. The Convention Center has a capacity for 1100 visitors. The motel/hotel accommodations consist of 950 units. Backing up the convention facilities are over 15 restaurants.

Compared to the Oregon coast, the real estate prices are relatively low. A lot on the beach front will cost $50,000 and up. Lots in the interior of the peninsula will go for as little as $10,000. Homes on Duck Lake and the canals range in cost from $80,000 up to the high $200,000s. Beach front homes can be found in the $150,000 range and up. Golf course homes sell for as little as $100,000.

Washington

The fire department provides the emergency care for the community. It has 8 full-time and 24 paid on-call personnel. In addition to this staffing, the community has an aid agreement with Grays Harbor (county) Fire District #7. The emergency care is provided by three advance life support ambulances and one ALS-equipped fire engine. Four of the career personnel are paramedic trained. 911 services are handled by the fire department.

The police department is made up of seven commissioned officers and six academy trained reserve officers. Besides the normal police duties these officers are also assigned surf rescue, scuba rescue and recovery team responsibilities. Two of the officers are also designated as U.S. Custom Agents. For a community of 2,800, the protection services appear to be quite adequate.

The Grays Harbor Community Hospital of Aberdeen has a clinic in the Ocean Shores community called the Coastal Care Clinic. This clinic operates 12 hours a day during the week and 8 hours on Saturdays. The staffing is provided by rotating specialists from the Grays Harbor Hospital. There is another medical clinic, slightly north of Ocean Shores, that also serves the community. It also provides for dental care. Crisis health services are augmented by hospitals in the larger communities of Aberdeen and Olympia.

Ocean Shores is a restful place. This is true most of the time but when the storms blow in off the north Pacific the tempo really picks up. This is a glorious place to be when the boiling and churning ocean meets the land and the bar at the mouth of Grays Harbor. The exhilaration of these storms is hard to describe. Many a frazzled big-city person will go to Ocean Shores in the winter to rejuvenate themselves by walking on the endless beach and experiencing the full fury of a Pacific storm. There is something renewing and invigorating about the crashing waves, the pelting rain and the powerful gusts of wind.

There are a lot of things to do at Ocean Shores. It is one of the premier bird watching areas on the Washington coast. Stream, lake, surf and deep sea fishing opportunities are readily available. To deep sea fish for salmon, cod and tuna, one need only cross the entrance of Grays Harbor to

Washington

Westport. The passenger ferry, El Matador, can handle that task quite handily. Westport is noted for its ocean sport fishing fleet.

The entrance to Grays Harbor, like many entrances to coastal rivers and harbors all up and down the West coast, has a bar and this results in very rough water. Many a sport fisherman has "lost his breakfast" going over the bar. The bar is no place for the amateur seaman!

Driving is allowed on the Ocean Shores beach. Mopeds and horses can be useful in exploring the beach and surrounding area. Beach combing, sand castle making and flying kites will keep the kids busy and happy. Wildlife abounds in the area. Besides the birds there are deer, seals, whales, raccoons , etc.

Ocean Shores is somewhat isolated. Seattle is 132 miles away, Aberdeen is 23 and Olympia is 72 miles away. The roads are good and the distance to the larger urban areas is reasonable for shopping trips, business, sport events and cultural opportunities.

Summary: Ocean Shores is attractive if one is retired, commutes rarely or is looking for a summer home. The services are more than adequate. There are lots of things to do, and for the occasional shopping trip to a larger community, the proximity is not bad. Real estate prices are low when compared to other places on the West coast. The summers are very nice and the winters are tolerable. Ocean Shores has the potential of being a real find and should be visited.

Kitsap Peninsula

The Kitsap Peninsula is west, across Puget Sound, from Seattle. Most people in Western Washington don't distinguish it from the Olympic Peninsula but it is a separate peninsula. It is bounded on the east side by Puget Sound and separated from the Olympic Peninsula, on the west, by Hood Canal. Kitsap County is the local governmental entity which overseas most of the Peninsula.

The economy of the Kitsap Peninsula is primarily supported by government installations. A large portion of the work force is employed by four naval installations, a large Naval shipyard and the Naval Hospital, both located in Bremerton, the Trident submarine program located at Bangor and the Naval Underwater Warfare Base at Keyport. It is estimated that about twenty thousand of the civilian work force is employed by the Navy. In addition to those employees, the military personnel number about 13,000.

There is always the possibility that the naval presence might grow because of the relocation of personnel and programs from other parts of the nation to the Puget Sound area. On the other side of that coin, there is also the possibility that the federal trend to downsize the military might reach the Puget Sound area. With these uncertainties always in mind, the county and cities are aggressively seeking diversification to decrease their dependence on the military.

The Peninsula has only four incorporated communities: Bremerton, Port Orchard, Poulsbo and Bainbridge Island. These cities account for 30% of the population. Kitsap County government deals with the task of governing the other 70%.

The weather of the area is primarily marine. The Olympic Mountains "rain shadow" has some influence in the northern part of the Peninsula, but it fades fast by the time one reaches the southern portion. For example, Hansville, in the north, receives 20 inches of precipitation annually. Port Orchard, in the south, receives 50 inches of precipitation a year.

The winters are rainy and generally mild in temperature. Snow is rare, the 1995 and 1996 winters were recent exceptions. On both occasions considerable snow visited the area. Normally when it does snow, it doesn't remain long. The summers really start in July and usually last through September. The summers are very pleasant, the temperatures are mild, and "sticky" humidity is rare.

The Kitsap Peninsula is a boater's dream. Puget Sound lies to the east. The shoreline is dotted with many small coves where the green forest comes down to the water's edge. Communities along the shoreline have large modern marinas which welcome transient boaters. Hood Canal, on the west, is another large body of water friendly to the boater. On the Canal, a boater might have an occasion to spot a giant Trident submarine returning after months at sea or possibly a whale - both are truly impressive sight.

Washington

Fishing, clamming, crabbing and harvesting oysters are all part of life in these beautiful water ways. Now and then a pod of "Killer Whales" or a giant Gray Whale comes for a visit.

The scenery is grand! Beside the water vistas, the snow-capped Olympic Mountains, the verdant forest, and neat farms, one can, on a clear day, take in the majestic beauty of Mt. Rainier located 60 - 65 miles to the southeast.

Three communities, Port Orchard, Silverdale and Poulsbo, were visited. (Two other communities, that are incorporated, were not visited but certainly are worthy of mention. They both have something to offer. Bainbridge Island is becoming a suburban community for Seattle. The commuter has a 20 to 30 minute ferry ride to Seattle - time for a coffee and a newspaper. The island is beautiful and the real estate is somewhat more expensive than in many of the surrounding communities. Bremerton is the largest city on the Olympic Peninsula. The shipyards are the major employer. Bremerton has many cultural amenities and the health services are very good. Real estate is considerably less expensive in Bremerton than in much of the Kitsap Peninsula.)

Port Orchard (5,600 Pop.)

Port Orchard is a small community across Sinclair Inlet from the larger community of Bremerton. Port Orchard is the county seat of Kitsap County. It is an incorporated community and its businesses and services are used by much of south Kitsap County. The growth of Port Orchard was about 13% for the period of 1990 - 1993. This area has been, and is expected to be, one of the faster growing areas in the state.

The natural environment of this area is typical of much of the Puget Sound. Port Orchard is on the water and is surrounded by rolling hills and deep green fir and cedar forests. The weather is marine which means that in the winter it rains but it rarely snows. The summers are mild and quite pleasant. The rain is less frequent in the summer, but enough to keep things green and fresh.

The economy of Port Orchard is dependent on the Bremerton shipyards and other military installations, plus the

Washington

commuters to Seattle. Port Orchard is one of the terminuses of the Washington State Ferry System.

Port Orchard and the surrounding area is growing but there is still room for new construction. Homes are reasonably priced. For example, a good three bedroom/two bath home can be purchased for $150,000 and up. Many of these homes will have a view of the water. Lots in the $50,000 to $100,000 range have water views.

The community has aggressive police and fire services. 911 service is available. For areas outside of Port Orchard, the county handles police and fire protection.

The local school district is a good size (10,000 + pupils) and has a reputation for providing a good education for the children of the community. It should also be mentioned that the school district provides many recreational and educational opportunities for the community. The high school has a state-of-the-art performing arts center and a 50 meter indoor swimming pool - all available to the larger community.

Olympic Community College (7,100+ students), in nearby Bremerton, provides many higher education opportunities for the folks in the community. From time to time, some of the state's four year institutions provide extension courses.

Medical services are good in Port Orchard. Group Health Cooperative, a large managed care organization in Washington, provides a priority medical care clinic. In close by Bremerton, Harrison Memorial Hospital provides sophisticated medical services to a good deal of Kitsap County, including Port Orchard. In addition, Port Orchard will, in the near future, be getting a substation of the Harrison Memorial Hospital.

Much of Port Orchard's cultural and entertainment amenities are augmented by Bremerton, Seattle and Tacoma. By car, Bremerton is 20 minutes away and Tacoma is 30 minutes away. Seattle is a 25 minute ferry ride away. Downtown Seattle, depending on the time of day, is 20 minutes by car from the ferry terminal in West Seattle.

The community sponsors a large number of festivals and fun activities. The one that tickles most peoples' fancy is a festival called "The Sea Gull Calling Festival." (Yes, you guessed right, like hog calling in the Midwest, these folks call

Washington

sea gulls - sounds like fun , doesn't it?) Other "noteworthies" are: Fathoms of Fun, On The Water Boat Show, Old Fashion Days, Chris Craft Rendezvous, Cruz - a custom car show , Christmas Lane Days and The Mosquito Fleet Days. If one likes antiques, dolls and dollhouse furniture then Port Orchard should have appeal.

The Mosquito Fleet Days refers to days gone by when a fleet of small boats moved freight and passengers from town to town along the shores of Puget Sound. Today this service is provided by the Washington State Ferry System. This System is one of the largest ferry systems in the nation.

For the person who likes to play golf, Port Orchard will be attractive. It has four nearby golf courses. One of the most outstanding courses is McCormick Woods which also plays host to an attractive residential development. It is possible, except for a few days, to golf year around in this part of Washington.

This region is a good place to live for the boating and fishing enthusiasts. Besides the salmon of the Puget Sound, the lakes of the region provide rainbow trout. Boating on Puget Sound is like having your own personal ocean at your front door.

The proximity of Port Orchard is ideal. It is very close to three relatively large urban areas. Port Orchard has a small private airport and Bremerton National can handle business jets and smaller planes. The close-by Seattle/Tacoma International Airport handles the bulk of the commercial traffic for the Puget Sound area.

Summary: The marine climate, although mild year around, is rainy during the winter. Cultural and entertainment amenities are readily available. Real estate is reasonable. The schools are good and generally well supported. Unemployment is low relative to other areas in the state and nation. Certainly, the beauty of the natural environment and the recreational opportunities are a big plus. It is a definite possibility and should be further investigated if one wants to live in the Pacific Northwest.

Washington

Silverdale (14,000 Pop.)

Silverdale is an unincorporated city and has the largest shopping center on the peninsulas. It is a fast growing bedroom community. One get the impression that everything is new. The area has experienced a tremendous growth in the last decade.

The Silverdale area has a great deal of natural beauty. The community is on Dyes Inlet, which for lack of a better description looks like a large bay. The green fir tree, the backbone of the logging industry, is all around. The inlet and sound is superb for boating. Snow-capped mountains are to the west and beautiful Mount Rainier is visible to the southeast.

Like all communities on the Kitsap Peninsula, Silverdale is supported primarily by federal government installations. A large modern retail sector is located in Silverdale and is important to the economy of the area. This sector is supported by shoppers from all over the peninsulas - Kitsap and Olympic. In recent years, cross-sound commuting has doubled in the Kitsap and Silverdale area. Like the rest of the Kitsap County, unemployment is low.

A good portion of the homes in this area will be less than ten years old. During the period of 1980 to 1990 the Silverdale population more than doubled. Even with this great increase in the population, the prices for housing have remained reasonable. A nice three bedroom/two bath home can be found for $125,000. View homes start around $180,000 and waterfront homes can be purchased for $300,000 and up. Non-view lots are available starting at $30,000. View lots start at $90,000 and waterfront lot will start at $150,000. Good waterfront property generally runs at $2,000 per linear foot.

Silverdale, although not incorporated, has many amenities. The schools are award winning and well supported. The county supplies police and fire protection. Utilities are reasonable when compared with the nation. Olympic Community College provides 2 year and 4 year degree programs. The college also provides a Work Force Training Program.

Health care is good and in the process of improving. Multi Care, the parent firm is Tacoma General Hospital, is building a 15 million dollar medical park. Harrison Memorial

Hospital has purchased 37 acres for a new hospital building. Of course, 911 is available.

The proximity of Silverdale, and all of Kitsap County for that matter, is very good. Seattle is 30 minutes away by ferry. Tacoma is 45 minutes away by road and Bremerton is 10 minutes away. These larger urban areas augment the cultural and entertainment opportunities, plus they provide many employment opportunities for the people of the Kitsap Peninsula.

Summary: Because of the beauty of the area, convenience of shopping, recreation, future medical services, good schools, real estate affordability and proximity, this is an area well worth consideration.

Poulsbo (4,900 Pop.)

Poulsbo is a unique little community at the head of Liberty Bay. The Olympic Mountains are to the west and their snow-capped splendor is a treat to the eye. To the southeast, one can view the magnificent beauty of the mountain giant, called Mt. Rainier. Poulsbo is a clone of a small Scandinavian village. Front Street is decked out in a Scandinavian decor. The "apotek" is busy dispensing medicine for the town folk and the "blomster buttek" is making up bouquets for an upcoming wedding. The baking smells of the famous Poulsbo bread often drift over the Bay. Boats, coming in off the Sound via Agate Pass, often bring their skippers and families to enjoy Poulsbo and its Scandinavian shopping opportunities.

This is a beautiful and unique community. Poulsbo's population is relatively young. It is a small community that is growing rapidly. Balance between growth and the intimacy of a small community is the goal in Poulsbo. Rainfall starts to decrease as one moves north on Kitsap Peninsula. Thirty-five inches is the average precipitation level in Poulsbo. The temperatures are mild year-around. During the winter, the temperatures run in the 40's while in the summer the temperatures will range in the 70's.

The economy, as with the rest of the Peninsula, relies greatly upon the federal installations. Commuters employed

Washington

in Seattle also enhance the community's economy. There is a big push to find businesses that will help diversify the economy.

Real estate prices appear to be relatively inexpensive. As one Realtor said, "There is something for everybody." Waterfront lots range from $150,000 up; waterfront homes will cost $325,000 and up; view lots can be purchased for $50,000 and up, with view homes going for $175,000 and up. Homes in town, with no view, start in the neighborhood of $90,000.

Poulsbo, like the other small communities of Kitsap Peninsula, relies on Harrison Memorial Hospital of Bremerton for hospital services. The community is incorporated and the fire and police departments are staffed with paid officers who are backed up by volunteers and reserve officers. 911 is available.

The schools of North Kitsap (Poulsbo) are good and large enough in enrollment to be able to provide a well rounded program. Unique to the community is the Marine Science Center. This is a center located on the waterfront in downtown Poulsbo. Its main purpose is to educate and inform. The school district, city and the center's association run the program.

Olympic Community College provides for higher education in the area and is intent on placing a branch in Poulsbo. North College of Art, a degree granting college that focuses on the arts, also provides educational opportunities.

Boating is big in Poulsbo. The town has 132 slips available. The Poulsbo Boat Rendezvous, during the month of July, is an annual gathering of Poulsbo built boats. Sea kayaking is also popular in the Bay and on the Sound where there are many little inlets to explore.. The Viking Festival, in May, is the big community festival which celebrates the Scandinavian heritage. This festival offers visitors the arts and crafts of the area. If one is particularly fond of lutesfisk there is always the October dinner held at the First Lutheran Church.

As for entertainment and sports, the Poulsbo folks can partake of the opportunities offered in Bremerton, Seattle and Tacoma. Like the rest of the Peninsula, larger urban areas are an easy commute away.

Washington

Summary: The weather is mild, recreation is plentiful, the schools are good, good health care is readily available, real estate prices are reasonable and availability is good. Poulsbo is an attractive community and should be of interest to someone looking for an alternative to the large urban community.

Olympic Peninsula

To the west of the Kitsap Peninsula one will find the Olympic Peninsula. This is a very large area that has some unusual properties. For example, you can be in a rain forest with over 220 inches of annual precipitation and drive a short distance and the land has to be irrigated. The Olympic Mountains cause the bulk of the Pacific marine moisture moving east to be dropped on the west side of the mountains. This condition creates a "rain shadow" effect on the east side of the mountains. Consequently, in the areas to the northeast and east of the mountains it is relatively dry - 13 to 20 inches. Port Angeles, Sequim, Port Townsend, Whidbey Island and the San Juan Islands all benefit from the "rain shadow". (In Western Washington low rainfall is considered desirable by many people.)

The Olympic National Park and Olympic National Forest make up about 75% of the Olympic Peninsula. The Olympic National Park has been designated as a World Heritage Site by the United Nations. There are only two such sites in the United States. Teddy Roosevelt established the Park in 1909 to protect the elk that bares his name - the Roosevelt elk. The Park is located in the center portion of the Peninsula and also has a 57 mile strip on the western coast. The national forest covers 640,000 acres and encircles the Park.

The Park boasts some of the largest trees in the world; the largest Alaskan Cedar, with a 37 feet diameter at the base, a Grand Fir and Western Hemlock, both measuring over 240 feet high, and a Douglas Fir reaching 300 feet above the forest floor. These giant trees are being protected and preserved for future generations.

The Strait of Juan de Fuca, Puget Sound, Hood Canal plus the Park and forest offer a variety of things to do. If one likes to hike, hunt, fish, ski, study a rain forest or just ponder

Washington

the majesty of the beautiful mountains, then the Olympic Peninsula is just the thing. If a drier climate and golf is a person's preference, then Sequim (Sqwim) will do. If one prefers boating and fishing, a relatively dry climate, and a beautiful shoreline, then Port Angeles, Port Townsend, and Port Ludlow are superb. Then, if a person is looking for isolation, a rugged coast, and great storms, then the Pacific coast portion of the Park is a super place.

Visits were made to Port Angeles, Sequim and Port Townsend, the largest incorporated communities on the Olympic Peninsula. Also visited was Port Ludlow, a community that is not incorporated but very nice and quite popular.

Port Ludlow (2,500 Pop.)

Now for something a little different. Port Ludlow started out as a resort with a golf course, a marina, restaurant and resort housing. It has now added a number of single family homes, condos, townhouses, a recreational center and an elegant inn.

It is a beautiful location with Hood Canal and Puget Sound on the east and the Olympic Mountains on the west. A 'snugly' harbor provides protection for the 300 slip marina. The residences are clustered in villages interspersed among the giant fir treed forest and a beautiful golf course.

When it comes to business and industry, there is only the resort and a few retail stores. Most of the permanent residents are either retired or commute to the larger cities of the Kitsap Peninsula, Seattle or Port Townsend. Travel time to the Kitsap Peninsula is 30 to 40 minutes and to Seattle, by ferry, it takes less than one and a half hours. Port Townsend is about 20 to 30 minutes to the north. There are a number of home owners who are 'weekenders' for the present but when they retire, they plan to become permanent residents. The community is very popular with retirees.

Real estate prices are surprisingly reasonable, considering its desirableness. Townhouses, condos and single family homes will start at about $150,000 and go to the low $300 thousands. The construction is relatively new and quite handsome.

Port Ludlow is in Jefferson County and relies upon the county for police and fire protection. 911 service is available from the county government. The Chimacum School District provides public education for the young people. Less than 20 miles to the north is Port Townsend, which provides the bulk of the needed medical services for the community.

To spend any time in the larger urban centers one must rely on ferry traffic. Depending on the conditions and timing the ferry ride can consume 1 to 2 hours. Sea-Tac International Airport by road and ferry is, depending on traffic conditions, approximately 2 - 3 hours away.

Many of the recreational amenities of this unincorporated community are provided by the newer two million dollar recreation center. This center provides the residents with an auditorium, a swimming pool, exercise rooms, arts, crafts and woodworking spaces as well as a place to hold lectures, dance and dine. The resort has a first class restaurant and an elegant inn for guests, a 27 hole championship golf course, and a modern marina. Port Townsend and Seattle augment the community's cultural and entertainment activities.

Summary: If golf, boating, fishing, or hiking are tops on ones list of activities, then Port Ludlow is a great place. The rainfall is certainly reasonable, 20 - 25 inches annually. Snow is rare and the summers are ideal. The isolation is not too great of a drawback considering the desirableness of Port Ludlow. If a person wants a place where there is great beauty, peace and quiet, fresh air and lots of activities, then Port Ludlow merits a serious look.

Port Townsend (7,000 Pop.)

Port Townsend is a fascinating place. It is one of the best examples of a Victorian seaport in the Pacific Northwest. You can almost imagine the harbor full of square-riggers from all over the world bringing their cargoes to the wharfs of Port Townsend. Many an unwary seaman was 'shanghaied' only to wake up on the deck of a ship headed for the Orient. The waterfront business district was filled with saloons and bordellos; so much so that those of a more genteel persuasion

Washington

established a separate business district on the hill above the waterfront business district.

There have been many changes in the life of the citizens of Port Townsend in the last 140 years but one thing that hasn't changed is the vitality the community. The Victorian architecture of the past still exist in many locations. In fact, over 70 buildings in Port Townsend are on the National Registry. Culturally and historically Port Townsend has become a modern-day "El Dorado".

The economy of the community is primarily dependent on the pulp and paper mill that is just south of the downtown business section. Boat repair and building also add to the prosperity of the community. Admiral Marine, a boat building company, is capable of designing and building very large yachts.

An interesting outgrowth of this focus on boats is the Northwest School of Boat Building. This school concentrates on the development of traditional boat building skills. The course is six months and the school produces some fine crafts persons for the boat repair and building businesses of the area.

In addition to the above, the community profits from a large tourist industry. This is primarily because of the interesting historical background of Port Townsend and its rich cultural climate. Unemployment during the winter runs about 9% but things pick up during the warmer months.

Real estate prices are not inexpensive. Many find this to be a very desirable place to live and the prices of homes reflect this. A three bedroom/two bath home in Port Townsend will sell for $130,000 up to $500,000. The price depends on location. Waterfront and view homes with beach access will cost a buyer $300,000 and up. Property with the same features outside of town can be purchased for less.

There are a number of Victorian homes in the area. Some have been turned into attractive bed and breakfast inns. Inns with acceptable locations will start at $300,000 and go up quickly beyond $500,000. If a person is interested in B&B's it is wise to secure the services of a Realtor who specializes in this part of the market. Also, remember when dealing with real estate, location is everything. This is particularly true in B&B's.

Property taxes are not particularly high in Port Townsend - approximately $1250 per $100,000 of assessed valuation.

There is a small hospital in Port Townsend which was recently expanded. It is capable of taking care of most of the needs of the community and surrounding area. Medical helicopter service is available. The more critical cases or cases requiring specialized services are transported to larger hospitals in the Seattle area.

The police and fire departments are staffed with a nucleus of paid staff backed up with reserve officers and volunteers. 911 is available in the community. The school system has an enrollment of 1,800 and is considered to be good. Washington State University and Peninsula Community College offer extension courses to the people of the community.

This is a vibrant cultural community. A number of artists, writers, musicians, and craft persons call Port Townsend home. Many professional people have retired to the area. This clustering of talent has given Port Townsend a healthy appetite for the arts.

This small community, of 7,000 citizens, supports over 17 galleries, and puts on many festivals and conferences dealing with the arts and history of the area. To provide a few examples, there is the Writers' Conference, the Feature Film Conference, the Classic Car Show, the Wooden Boat Festival, the American Fiddle Tunes gathering, Port Townsend Chamber Music, Port Townsend Blues Festival and the Kinetic Sculpture Race. (This last item deals with racing people-powered vehicles.)

A nonprofit organization called "Centrum" is responsible for the promotion of the arts and creative education. This organization brings many of the artistic and cultural events to Port Townsend.

The community has some wonderful performing facilities. Fort Worden, originally built in 1896 for the protection of Puget Sound, has been turned into a state park. That site now includes the 1,400 seat Mc Gurdy Pavilion and the smaller Fort Worden Theater.

The fact that Port Townsend gets 18 inches of precipitation makes it an ideal area for outdoors recreation. Kayaking,

Washington

sailing, fishing, golf, crabbing, clamming, hiking, hunting are all popular.

Port Townsend is perhaps two hours, via ferry, from Seattle and one hour from Silverdale and the Kitsap Mall. It is on the edge of the Olympic National Park and not far from the Canadian city of Victoria. The trip to Victoria can be made in 2 or 3 hours and costs are reasonable. The ferry leaves from Port Angeles, which is a short distance from Port Townsend.

Summary: Port Townsend has everything to offer a person looking for a community that values the arts and it historical background. Real estate is not the least expensive in the Pacific Northwest but with some looking a buyer can get good value. The weather is good - little or no snow, the proximity isn't too bad and the cultural vitality of the community is exciting. This is a must see community for someone looking for an exciting place to live in the Pacific Northwest.

Sequim (4,000 Pop.)

The next community to visit is just up the road from Port Townsend. Sequim (Skwim) makes one think that they are in Southern California or Utah. This is a small town located in the beautiful Dungeness Valley. Just four miles to the north is the Strait of Juan de Fuca and to the south are the majestic Olympic Mountains and the Olympic National Forest.

There are places on the Olympic Peninsula, less than 30 miles away from Sequim, that get in excess of 200 inches of precipitation annually. In Sequim, because of the mountains "rain shadow", the rainfall is only 16 inches, making it one of the drier spots in Washington. It is a sunny place, with over 300 days of sunshine. Temperatures range from a summer high of 88 degrees to a winter low in the high teens. Sometimes a dip to the minus degrees is experience but not often. Sequim is a favorite for retirees.

The economy is driven primarily by agriculture. In the late 1800's, the farmers started to irrigate with the waters of the Dungeness River. The river waters brought life to the very dry soil and ever since, it has been a farming and dairy area. Tourism is also helpful to the economy and certainly the many retirement checks received by the residents help stabilize the economy.

Highway 101 passes through the community on the main street and in the summer time traffic can get quite heavy. A bypass is under development to help alleviate the traffic situation. To the east of town, on the Indian reservation, the 7 Cedars Casino is located. This enterprise brings a number of job opportunities to the local residents. (In Washington a number of Indian reservations have gone into the "gaming" business. The casinos appear to be quite popular, well managed, and regulated.)

Homes in the area range in cost from the low $100,000s and up. A new three bedroom/two bath home with a double garage can be purchased for as little as $112,000. Small waterfront homes start in the low $200,000s. Golf course homes will run in the high $100,000s. View properties can start in the mid $100,000s and go up to the $600,000s. Many of the view properties come with small acreages. Bell Hill, which is immediately south of town, has very nice homes that can be found in the $300,000s and up. The view from Bell Hill is, to quote the kids, "awesome". You can see the Strait, snow-capped Mt. Baker and the Cascades, and at night the lights of Victoria, British Columbia.

Police and fire services, as with many towns of this size, have some full-time paid staff but still must rely partially on reserve officers and volunteers. A 911 program is in operation. Because of the high number of retirees, medical and dental practitioners are well represented in the community. Olympic Memorial Hospital, located in nearby Port Angeles, is used for hospitalization. For extreme health cases the hospitals in the Seattle area support the Port Angeles hospital.

The schools are good. The public schools have an enrollment of slightly less than 3,000 students. The community in 1996 passed a 25 million dollar school construction bond. The town has a good library and extension courses are available from Western Washington University and Peninsula Community College. Bus service is available within the town and to Port Townsend and Port Angeles. Sequim has an airport that can handle private planes and commuter flights are handled

Washington

at Port Angeles. A shuttle can be taken to the Sea-Tac International Airport.

There are, besides its climate, some other unique features about Sequim. The Olympic Game Farm is located nearby. This farm has trained a number of animals that are seen in Hollywood productions. Obviously boating is popular in this area. John Wayne use to spend some time here on his boat the, "Wild Goose". The John Wayne Marina is located just to the east of town in the Sequim Bay. This marina has 444 slips and 22 guest slips. The Strait of Juan de Fuca is a giant body of water which makes for good sailing and power boating, as well as wind surfing, kayaking, fishing, clamming, and crabbing. Hunting is good in the national forests, but is not allowed in the Olympic National Park. The town is located on relatively flat terrain and biking can be enjoyed. Not to be forgotten are two golf courses. Sunland is a nearby community that has a golf course surrounded by residences.

Special mention should be given to the Dungeness Spit. The Spit forms a seven mile crescent which provides a protected area for the Dungeness National Wildlife Refuge. It is one of the longest spits in the world.

In addition to the outdoor features, the community has some cultural pursuits that can add to the quality of life. Besides the extension courses and the good library, the community has a little theater group and a new cultural and art center is in the works.

Port Angeles is 17 miles to the west of Sequim, while Port Townsend is about 30 miles to the east and slightly north. Seattle and Victoria are both a couple of hours away by car and ferry.

Summary: This small community is a fascinating place, partly because of the unique climatic environment and partly because there are so many recreational and cultural activities. It is a community that is relaxed and displays a healthy enthusiasm for life and community involvement. The people of the community display an openness which reflects the fact that the residents come from many places. For a person who enjoys a lot of sun and changes in the seasons, this is a grand place. If a person is looking for a retirement place in a beautiful part of the country, then Sequim should be on the list of places to check out.

Port Angeles (17,700 Pop.)

Port Angeles is considered the "Gateway to Olympic National Park". It is located on the Strait of Juan de Fuca and the Olympic National Park is directly south of the community. G. Scott Thomas, in his book, *Rating Guide to Life in America's Small Cities*, ranked Port Angeles 7th out of 219 communities examined in the United States. This honor appears to be well deserved. The city has a great deal to offer and is very popular with retirees. It is located in an area with some of the most beautiful scenery in the world and has many outstanding cultural and recreational opportunities available for its residents.

Three large mills that produce plywood, paper and pulp are critical to the economy of Port Angeles. Being at the beginning of the Strait of Juan de Fuca, the town offers many boating services for the private and commercial boat owner. The Arthur D. Furo Marine Laboratory, which is run by the local college, operates in Port Angeles. Commercial fishing is also pursued in the area and a new pier for commercial fish processing is available. Ediz Hook, a mile long sand spit, provides Port Angeles a nice protected harbor. Ediz Hooks also provides a site for the United States Coast Guard Station which is one of the larger employer in Port Angeles. The community is experiencing an increase in the immigration of small businesses.

Real estate prices are reasonable when compared to many communities in the country. For example, a nice three bedroom/two bath home can be purchased for $150,000. Good homes with splendid view can be found for $200,000. Good view acreage plots will run a buyer in the neighborhood of $50,000 to $60,000. Homes with multiple acreage start around $180,000. Lots in town can be found in the $30,000 to $40,000 range "maxing out" at around $80,000. Waterfront lots will cost $100,000 and up. Considering the attractiveness of some of the parcels, the prices seem quite reasonable when compared to the larger urban areas of Washington and Oregon and

Washington

the Oregon coast. While on the subject of real estate, the tax rate is approximately $1,450 per $100,000 of assessed valuation.

Port Angeles has good community services. The police department has 43 employees. The fire department is staffed by 18 full-time employees and backed-up by 22 volunteers. Medic One has one of the fastest response times in the nation. Olympic Memorial Hospital is a 126 bed facility. It is staffed with 63 physicians. The hospital was rated among the best in the state of Washington by the Washington State Hospital Association. Cases requiring specialized treatment such as heart surgery or critical burns are sent to Seattle.

Fairchild International Airport has 2 runways and a passenger terminal. It is served by Horizon Air, a commercial commuter carrier.

The public school enrollment is 5,200 students. Such an enrollment allows for a broad curricular program. The community's support of the schools is good. Peninsula Community College provides an associate degrees. City University, a private four year institution, is also present in the community.

When it comes to cultural and recreational pursuits, Port Angeles is outstanding. The 60 year old Port Angeles Symphony has been invited to perform in China, Peru and Bolivia. This is a real testimony to the quality of their program. Port Angeles also has a light opera troupe, a community theatrical group, summer concerts on the pier, a Fine Arts Center and a community Festival of Arts which focuses on visual arts, music, drama, dance and crafts. A community concert association annually arranges a series of live concerts by nationally and internationally known performers.

Recreation abounds in the Port Angeles area. The Olympic National Park allows for hiking, wildlife viewing, skiing at Hurricane Ridge and fishing for the Beardslee trout, which can weigh up to 16 pounds. Within one hour from the city a person can find some of the best fishing in the nation on one of twelve rivers and many lakes. Of course, the Strait provides fishing for salmon, halibut and other bottom fish. Clamming and crabbing are also available. Boating is quite popular in the area.

Washington

Hunting is available in the Olympic National Forest. There are opportunities for biking along the trails, golfing at the Peninsula Golf Club, which is open to the public, and tennis is available at some of the parks.

Port Angeles might appear to be quite a distance from the larger urban areas but the roads are good and the times are reasonable. Seattle by road and ferry is about 2-3 hours away, the Kitsap Mall is only 1-1/2 hours away. The fascinating city of Victoria, B.C. is 55 minutes away on the passenger ferry that crosses the Strait of Juan de Fuca.

Summary: This little city is sometimes called the "City of Flowers". During the summer you will find baskets full of flowers all up and down the main streets and on the waterfront. The climate is a mild marine climate, the rainfall is less than 25 inches and snowfall is either very little or none at all. Temperatures will run in the 70's in the summer and in the 30's and 40's in the winter. Cultural and recreational opportunities abound. The services of the community are very good. The beauty of the waters and the mountains is magnificent This is a place to look over if you want a stimulating and pleasant cultural and natural environment.

Northwestern Washington

This is the region just south of the Canadian border and on the east side of Puget Sound. There are two major components, the San Juan Islands and the mainland.

The San Juan Islands are composed of 175 small islands with only 60 inhabited. The islands are like little pieces of jade scattered on a carpet of blue velvet. They have green forests, small neat fields, cozy coves and lots of boats. This is a sailor's paradise. Navigation in among the islands is relatively easy but one must always cast a watchful eye for the giant ferries that plow these lovely waters.

Since the 80's the islands' population has experienced sizable growth. They have about 12,500 permanent residents. These islands are popular with tourists and retirees. Tourism, retirement income and some farming provide the economic base for the islands. Real estate is generally expensive.

Washington

The mainland has many similar features, only in greater magnitude. It is a beautiful place also. It has giant forests of Douglas fir, cedar and hemlock. A number of swift rivers rush down from the mountains to meet the sea. This is the home of the gorgeous daffodil and tulip fields so popular with calendar and magazine covers. Snow-capped Mt. Baker and the majestic Cascades are always within sight and there is the always the presence of the sea.

Growth has impacted the mainland and it continues to this day. One distinct difference between the two areas of the region is that the mainland doesn't have to rely upon ferry service to get home. Of course, there are those that think the reliance upon the ferries is part of the excitement of living on an island—different strokes for different folks.

In this part of the world timber and wood products, fishing, agriculture, oil refineries, retail enterprises and tourism are the main economic drivers. Retirees are also starting to provide additional stability to the economy. Real estate is reasonable but certainly not inexpensive.

The weather is definitely marine but it has some surprises. The Olympic Mountains, to the west, have considerable impact on this area. These mountains form a "rain shadow" that makes the climate much dryer than one would expect. The average rainfall for this area will range from the low teens to about 35 inches. It is a fact, the island of San Juan is even dryer and has cactus growing on it. This island is one of the sunniest spots in Washington. This is quite a surprise for the folks who think that all it does in Western Washington is rain - definitely not the case in this part of Western Washington.

This region is a recreational playground, especially if boating and fishing is a person's passion. The islands, as well as the mainland coast, provide all sorts of coves to anchor in during the night. A fresh caught salmon on the grill with some crabs in the pot makes for a wonderful dinner under the star-filled sky. The mountains are close by and present amply opportunities for countless adventures at hiking, camping, fishing, hunting, whitewater rafting, climbing, downhill and cross country skiing, snowmobiling, etc.

The two communities visited, Anacortes and Bellingham, possess many of the features characteristic of this region. They provide beginning points for island or mountain exploration and possess a population large enough to have good community services.

The islands are fascinating and if one sees them as a possibility, they certainly should be on the itinery when visiting this region. For the purpose of this discussion they have not been included.

Anacortes (12,800 Pop.)

Anacortes is located on Fidalgo Island. A person going to Anacortes would never realize that he is on an island. It is a narrow waterway called the Swinomish Channel that separates Fidalgo from the mainland and classifies it as an island.

Anacortes is a jumping off spot for the San Juan Islands and a number of "Anacortesians" like to think of themselves as part of the San Juan archipelago but in reality Fidalgo is not part of the chain, at least from the indications on the map.

The community is clean and neat and with fabulous vistas of water, cozy coves, forests, and mountains. One can not avoid being struck by the almost Scandinavian appearance of the area. The town occupies a series of low hills and the homes, which for the most part are well kept, are inviting. The folks of Anacortes are friendly and quite proud of their community and its accomplishments.

Artisans have found Anacortes quite appealing. One of the most famous residents of Anacortes was Burl Ives. It is a peaceful beautiful place which holds great appeal to many folks with the creative bent. Retirees looking for a more simple lifestyle have also found the community to their liking.

The economy is driven by the refineries to the east. The oil from the fields of Alaska is refined at these installations. Other economic drivers are boat building, fishing, log loading, retail and commercial enterprises, some agriculture, ferry service and tourism.

Anacortes' proximity to the islands, boating opportunities and appealing natural environment has drawn folks to the area. A new three bedroom/two bath home can be found in the mid $100,000 range. A 9,000 sq. ft. lot with a water and

Washington

island view will sell in the $90,000 range. A large newly constructed home, with real territorial views, can be found in the $300,000 range and up.

One interesting thing which was noticed when visiting the community was there were several newer homes that had been built to reflect the architectural style of the 20's and 30's. Also, several of the newer homes reflected the traditional farmhouse styles popular in bygone days. These styles in new construction appeared to be unique to Anacortes and were found to be quite refreshing.

The community has professional police and fire protection. 911 is available. The Island Hospital, a 43 bed facility, services the community and at times folks from the islands. It is backed-up by hospitals in Seattle or nearby Mt. Vernon (that is Washington not Virginia).

The public schools are relatively small (2,950 enrollment). They do, however, provide a comprehensive program and are recognized for their excellence.

A publicly supported bus transportation system called Skagit Transportation services Skagit County and Anacortes. The Anacortes Airport has a runway of 3,000 feet and the airport services private aircraft. A small commercial commuter service is available from the airport. For national or international flights either Sea-Tac or Vancouver B. C. can provide such service. A van shuttle service is available for Sea-Tac.

For a small community Anacortes has a lot to offer the person who is interested in the arts. The community has a number of artist, writers, poets, craft persons who call this place home. These folks have considerable influence on the cultural and entertainment climate of the community. One thing that can not escape the attention of a visitor is the large number of buildings with murals. There are 65 murals, mostly appearing in the downtown area. These murals depict some events or persons who have had some historical impact on the community.

Anacortes has a community theatrical group. Brodniak Hall, a 806 seat performing arts center, provides facilities for many community events. The Skagit Symphony gives a number of community performances.

Washington

Since boating is so important to the community, an event to celebrate the opening of boating season is a must. The Waterfront Festival in May serves this purpose. They also have the Art Festival in August, a "judged" show and throughout the year they have art walks.

History and art are important to the community. To backup their support of the arts they have turned the old railroad station into a historical museum and art gallery.

The Tulip Festival celebrates the spring blooming of the tulip in the Skagit Valley. If a person has not visited the tulip field in the Skagit Valley in the spring, then they have missed one of the most beautiful sights in the world.

There are a number of other events that demonstrate the personality of the community, e.g., book sales, quilt shows, home and boat tours, and the 4th of July celebration. If one absolutely must have more, then Seattle and its rich cultural and entertainment environment is available 80 miles to the south.

Recreation revolves around the outdoors. Anacortes has set aside 2,200 acres of forest land as a reserve. It has hiking and bike trails, view points and wonderful examples of the flora and fauna of the Pacific Northwest.

Boating is big in Anacortes. There are five large excellent marinas with 1000s of boats. A number of Seattlites have moorage in Anacortes. Its proximity to the San Juans makes it an ideal moorage place for adventurous mariners. Where there are boats there is fishing and Anacortes is big on fishing.

The mountains, to the east, provide for skiing, backpacking, hiking, mountain climbing, hunting and all sorts of other activities associated with mountain terrain.

Anacortes is comfortably located near large urban areas. Seattle is 80 miles to the south and Vancouver B.C. is about the same distance to the north.

Summary: Anacortes has a natural beauty that is very appealing. The town has good protection services, the schools are first class and hospital services are more than adequate. Real estate prices are slightly higher than one would like. They still are a bargain when considering the larger urban areas of Seattle, Portland and San Francisco. The economy is stable and

Washington

the large retiree population and the refineries help maintain this stability. Culturally, the community is rich and recreationally the proximity to the sea, islands and mountains, provide outdoor activities that are superb.

All-in-all, Anacortes has a lot to offer someone who is a boater, a retiree or has a creative bent. When one is heading north on Interstate 5 and you've gone through Mt. Vernon, take a left on Highway 20 and visit Anacortes—you won't be sorry.

Bellingham (57,700 Pop.)

Bellingham is a city of hills, forests, lakes, mountains and the beautiful Bellingham Bay. It is located at the southern end of the Strait of Georgia and north of Puget Sound. The majestic Cascade Range forms the eastern backdrop for the community and the snow covered Olympic Range can be seen far across the waters to the southwest.

The commercial section of the community has built up around the Bay. It is here that one finds, mixed in among newer structures, some beautiful old buildings that have been thoughtfully restored. The city has grown and like all cities, much that is new appears on the outskirts in the form of shopping centers, business parks and residential developments. Closer to downtown is the University with it wonderful campus. Western Washington University brings to the community much beauty and countless cultural, educational and entertainment opportunities.

The residential part of the community that is closer to the Bay is older but well kept and provides many opportunities for less expensive housing. Developments in the outer parts of the community provide contemporary housing opportunities. Bellingham homes have some views that are outstanding.

This is a city that was ranked, in 1995 by *Swing Magazine*, as one of the premier cities for young adults. The New York based Macmillan Travel, in 1995, ranked it the third best place to retire in the U.S. In 1994 *Money Magazine* ranked it second out of 20 top communities for entrepreneurs. It appears, according to the above, that both the young and older citizens like Bellingham and that it offers numerous opportunities for the "go-getters" in business.

The economy's drivers revolve around the University, pulp and paper, wood products, boat building, shipping and ferry service, education, medical treatment and tourism. Canadian business relocation to Bellingham has been strong. Since 1989 there have been 110 Canadian businesses moving to Bellingham. What attracts these businesses? The cost of doing business in the U.S. is generally lower and the tax structure is less burdensome. In addition to business relocations, the Canadians come to Bellingham to shop.

The slightly higher cost of housing in Bellingham can be partially explained by the fact that this is a university town as well as a very desirable place to live. A new three bedroom/two bath home will start in the mid $100,000 range and go up. View properties with a good house can be found in the upper $100,000 range and waterfront properties will be in the mid $200,000 range and up. There are a large number of less expensive homes that would be great candidates for refurbishment. If someone wants a house that is big, new and has a great view then one will find it in Bellingham, but it will cost in the four to five hundred thousand dollar range.

St. Joseph's Hospital is a full-service hospital. This is a big plus for living in this community. 911 is available. The city provides professional police and fire protection. Utility cost is comparatively low. Taxes are reasonable when compared to other parts of the country.

Education in this community is one of its highlights. The public schools, with an enrollment of 10,000, are nationally ranked as outstanding. *Expansion Magazine*, an international business magazine, ranked the schools as tops among the Washington schools it reviewed.

There are five institutions of higher learning in the community. Western Washington University is the largest and is located in the city. Whatcom Community College, and Northwest Indian College both provide programs for Associate Degrees. Bellingham Technical College provides technical training and City University, a private institution provides a four-year program.

Washington

In the area of transportation, Bellingham is the U.S. home to the Alaska Marine Highway System. This is a ferry service that serves Alaska with passenger and vehicle transportation. If one wants to use commercial air service then a trip to Sea-Tac International Airport or the Vancouver B.C. airport is necessary. There is a shuttle service to Sea-Tac.

Culturally, much of what Bellingham has to offer comes from the University. The University provides opportunities in ballet, music and dramatic performances. The town has a theater group called the Bellingham Theatre Guild. They are responsible for a number of very fine productions during the year. Of course, one should not forget the Whatcom Symphony and its wonderful programs. There are also art walks sponsored during the year. Bellingham appeals to artists and crafts persons.

The Whatcom Museum of History and Art is housed in the old city hall built in 1892. It is a beautiful structure that has been tastefully renovated. The building is bright red brick, and has a wonderful old fashion clock tower and it is a magnificent example of late 1800's architecture. When it comes to a performing arts center, few communities can match the restored 1,500 seat vaudeville theater called the Mt. Baker Theater.

Boating is one of the premier experiences of the Bellingham area. There is a large protected marina and boat building and repair services to fit the boater's needs are readily available. Going right along with boating is the fishing. This is an area where the salmon still hang out. Stream fishing is also good.

If one likes the mountains, then there are the Cascades with Mt. Baker at over 10,000 feet and its neighbor Mt. Shuksan. Skiing is popular at Mt. Baker and camping, hiking and mountain climbing are readily available.

Golf at Semiahmoo, a first class resort, is close-by and there are three other 18 hole courses in the vicinity. If baseball is one's game, there is a Class "A" team from the Giants organization that plays during the summer. The University is a great place to enjoy college sports.

One thing that captured the imagination of this writer was the famous Ski to Sea Festival. Besides the festive atmosphere of the town, there is a relay race from the mountains to the sea where there are seven activities, e.g. skiing, running, biking, swimming, etc. Sounds like great fun for the stout of heart.

Bellingham is 25 miles from the Canadian border. Vancouver, a fabulous city in British Columbia is about 56 miles north of Bellingham. Seattle is about two hours south of Bellingham.

Summary: Bellingham has a lot going for it. It is a community of unmatched natural beauty. The Bay and Sound, mountains, forests and lakes provide for a rich recreational environment. Culturally, it has an interesting history and a number of quality cultural activities. The city is large enough to support good city services, the schools are excellent, there are a number of institutions of higher learning and there is a full-service hospital. The economy is good and growing. The community has been nationally recognize as good for business, good for young folks and a place that is popular with retirees.

Bellingham is certainly worth strong consideration for a visit. It is on the road to Canada, so the next time on your way to Vancouver be sure to get off Interstate 5 and look around—it will be time well spent.

North Central Washington

The North Central Washington region includes Wenatchee and stretches to the north about 140 miles to the Canadian border. It includes the eastern slope of the Cascade Mountains and generally involves the Okanogan and Columbia valleys from the Canadian border down to Wenatchee.

This terrain reminds one of many parts of the southwest. It is relatively dry, has that "brown look" that goes with such climates. From the crest of the mountains down to the valleys, the pine trees grow fewer and fewer giving way to the willows and locust trees so prevalent in the semiarid regions. It is the waters from the valley's rivers that give life to the dry landscape. Fruit growing, wood products, power generation, some manufacturing and livestock provide the region's economic base.

Washington

Real estate is reasonable and the manufactured homes are accepted and numerous.* This type of housing is less expensive than a "stick built" home and faster to put up. With today's modern methods of construction, a manufactured house is a very adequate substitute for the more traditionally built house. Stick-built houses are still the predominate choice for housing in the region.

As for culture and entertainment, the smaller communities rely on rodeos, festivals and local talent. Wenatchee, the largest city in the region, serves as the cultural, entertainment, medical and commercial center for North Central Washington.

Recreation for the area focuses on the outdoors. The mountains, lakes and rivers provide a fabulous playground for the folks of the region. It is a place where many people from Western Washington come to enjoy the fishing and hunting. Boating is big on the lakes created by the dams on the Columbia River. Downhill and cross country skiing is available as is snowmobiling, hiking, camping, backpacking, and some prospecting.

The weather is warm in the summer and cold in the winter. Snow ventures down into the valleys on occasions but does not usually stop people from getting around. This is an area where there is plentiful sunshine.

North Central Washington is truly a Western region. Here a person will see loggers, cowboys and farmers. The trusty pickup truck with its standard gun rack, high heeled boots of the cowboy or wanna-be cowboy and the Stetson hat are all part of this region. If one is quick and looks real hard at the distant horizon then one might spot the "Marlboro Man" (minus his cigarette, hopefully) driving a unruly herd of "doggies".

A few words about manufactured houses: a person will find that manufactured houses are a fairly popular alternative to "stick-built" houses in North Central Washington. These houses are well built and insulated. The cost is about one-half the cost of a "stick-built" house. They appear to be a good answer to a vacation home or for that matter a permanent residence for those wanting less expensive housing. Of course, there are good points and bad points. Cost and time are two advantages that come readily to mind. Some possible draw back have to do with zoning, resale and plan flexibility.

Leavenworth (1,700 Pop.)

Leavenworth is a Bavarian-like village tucked away in the rugged Cascade Mountains. This is not an ethnic village but a revitalized community that has captured the imagination of the traveler by presenting a Bavarian motif and customs.

This was certainly not the case back in the 60's. Progress had passed them by and the town had become just another wide spot in the road from Seattle to Wenatchee. Two of the leading citizens of the community saw, that without something being done, the downward trend was not going to change. The University of Washington was contacted and a redevelopment plan was devised and set into action. The Bavarian theme was just the thing to capture the attention of the passersby. Slowly, but surely, the merchants and the people of the community set about reshaping the community. As money became available, the store fronts and interiors of the businesses were changed to capture the Bavarian motif. Festivals were developed that furthered the Bavarian atmosphere. Today, the village of Leavenworth is prospering and the tourists keep returning to enjoy the people and beauty of a "Bavarian" village.

The economy of the area is primarily dependent on the tourist trade but there are other enterprises such as timber and agriculture that influence the economy. The federal government is the largest land owner, with private timber companies being second. Consequently, land for housing is somewhat scarce. Leavenworth is a highly desirable area and the scarcity of land combined with demand, make the real estate prices higher than in other nearby communities. A newer three bedroom/two bath house will start at about $150,000 and can go up rapidly depending on location.

Some folks are buying older and smaller homes in town, remodeling or tearing them down, and building new. New building sites outside of town, with some acreage, will go for

Washington

$60,000 up to $100,000 depending on the location. The building cost start around $65 per square foot.

Slightly north of the downtown there is some new construction with territorial views of the town and surrounding mountains. An attractive 3,400 square foot new home on one acre had an asking price of $345,000. Condos are becoming more popular in the area. It is thought by some of the Realtors that this condo trend will continue to grow. Property taxes are running in the neighborhood of $2,000 per $100,000 of accessed value.

Police and fire services are contracted out to the county. The nationally accredited Cascade Medical Center has 33 beds and also supplies ambulance service for the community. Hospitals in Wenatchee and Seattle provide backup for critical cases.

The public school system is composed of five school buildings and has an enrollment in excess of 1,400. Wenatchee Community College is located 22 miles to the east. Central Washington University, located in Ellensburg, provides extension courses in Wenatchee.

The closest airport with commercial services is Panghorn Memorial Airport, 30 miles away in East Wenatchee. There is a local public bus service that is free and connects Leavenworth with Cashmere, Wenatchee, East Wenatchee, Entiat and Chelan. This allows the residents of Chelan County a convenient and inexpensive way to do their business, shopping and visiting. The bus service is funded by a county sales tax. Electrical rates in Leavenworth and Chelan County are some of the least expensive in the nation.

There are delightful festivals that take place in Leavenworth. The residents take great pride in making these occasions extremely attractive to the visitors. In keeping with the Bavarian theme, there is the Leavenworth International Accordion Celebration, the International Folk Dance Performance, Maifest (celebrating spring with its tuba oompas, singing and Bavarian dancers), the Bavarian Ice Fest and the very popular Christmas Tree Lighting Ceremony which draws people from all over Washington.

Icicle Creek Music Center opened in 1995. Guest artists from the over the world perform and instruct. The intent of the center is to present, "... a community where artists, audiences, and students can interact personally, sharing in the magic of the creative process..."

Recreation opportunities abound in the Leavenworth area. Skiing is available at Stevens Pass, 35 miles to the west. Leavenworth has a small hill on which a family can have a good time learning to ski and Mission Ridge is located in the mountains above Wenatchee. In the winter a person can enjoy snowmobiling, cross country skiing, snowshoeing, and dog sledding. In the summer there is backpacking, hiking, golf, fishing, boating on Lake Wenatchee, river rafting, bicycling, motor biking and horseback riding. In the fall, hunting is added to the above.

Speaking of weather, suffice it to say, the winters are cold but not unbearable, The summers are warm and pleasant. It snows over 1 inch about 30 days a year and a trace of rain is present about 18 days a year.

The proximity of Leavenworth is good. Wenatchee, a medium size city is within a reasonable distance. Seattle is 118 miles.

Summary: Leavenworth is a jewel. The Bavarian theme and the reliance upon visitors seems to give the community a common focus. Jobs are not numerous in the town. The tourist traffic, the life blood of the community, gets a little hectic at times. There are lots of thing to do to keep busy if someone is financially independent and wants to participate in the community activities. There are definitely four seasons. Utilities are very reasonable and taxes a bit high but not too bad when compared with many urban areas. The cost of housing is higher than in surrounding communities. All things considered, Leavenworth has much to offer.

Chelan (3,000 Pop.)

When does a person get the opportunity to live in an area designated as "Pristine?"

Lake Chelan is one of three areas in the United States having this designation. The city of Chelan is located at the eastern end of the fiord-like Lake Chelan. The western end of

Washington

the lake is remote, rugged and wild. The boat trip "uplake" is bordered by steep cliffs, cascades of pure mountain water, mountain goats and the North Cascade National Park. The bulk of the population resides at the eastern end of the lake.

The economy of the area is supported by fruit growing, fruit processing, and tourism. Chelan is famous for its apples. Between 9,000 and 10,000 acres of apple orchards are located in the area. The majority of the orchards are small and worked by families. A few orchards are owned by agricultural firms.

Tourism is promoted by the large number of resorts along the lake shore. Campbell's is the oldest of the resorts and is in the center of town. Their are a number of timeshare resorts, with Wapato Point being the largest. The new Indian casino, in nearby Manson, is also attracting visitors.

Newer homes in the Chelan area start in the mid $100,000s. Of course, there are some less expensive homes that are smaller and older and lend themselves to remodeling. Waterfront homes can be purchased in the mid $200,000 range but the bulk of available waterfront homes cost $300,000 and up. Waterfront lots run from the low of $100,000 to the upper $200,000s. View properties come in two types, community beach access and just views of the lake and mountains. View lots, with community beach access, will range from the $70,000s to the low $100,000s. A view lot, without beach access, will range in price from $50,000 to the low $100,000s.

The town of Manson, a short distance up the lake from Chelan, has properties somewhat less expensive than Chelan. Also, at Manson is the beautiful timeshare and single family community of Wapato Point. This is leased land form the local Indian tribe. There are some gorgeous single family residences with outstanding views of the lake and mountains at prestigious Wapato Point.

The Chelan police department is manned by paid officers and the fire department is a volunteer organization. The public education system provides a strong basic education program. There are approximately 1,200 pupils enrolled in the schools.

A small private plane airport is located to the north of town. It has a 3,570 foot runway and provides rental, tie-down

Washington

spaces. The nearest commercial airport is Panghorn Memorial Airport at East Wenatchee. The free, Link bus transportation system is always available to scoot a person off to Wenatchee or even Leavenworth for shopping and business. There are two ferries which carry passengers and freight up the lake to Stehekin and Holden Village.

The Lake Chelan Community Hospital provides for much of the health care for the valley. It provides a full compliment of services. It services are augmented by the larger hospitals in Wenatchee, Spokane and Seattle. A 911 system is available.

The culture and entertainment of the community is pretty much self contained. A newer performing arts facility is available. There is an active theater group that produces some fine shows. There is dinner theater at one of the resorts and a number of opportunities to enjoy community concerts. Lake Chelan Bach Fest is an impressive affair as is the Riverwalk Fine Arts Exhibit. There are a number of galleries that display local and outside art. If a person can not find something that is appealing, then Wenatchee and its entertainment and cultural menu is always available.

What else is there to do in Chelan? There is fishing for the Lake Chelan salmon and trout. Hunting is good. Cross country and downhill skiing, cycling, hiking, snowmobiling, snowshoeing, boating, whitewater rafting, water skiing, rodeo, World Championship Hang Glider aerobatics, golf and a casino are all available for one's pleasure.

Chelan has 300 days of sunshine, wonderful restful Indian summers, cold winters but not too cold, glorious springs with the fruit tree blossoms and warm sunny summers. Most of the area's moisture comes in the winter months in the form of snow. The summers are dry. It is easy to see why Lake Chelan draws folks from Western Washington who need that vital "hit" of sunshine.

The Lake itself is magnificent! It is 55 miles long and 1 to 2 miles wide. It is located in one of the deepest gorges in the United States. Its depth is 1,486 feet and it is the third deepest lake in the United States - Crater Lake and Lake Tahoe are deeper. The lake's depth will drop by 20 feet during the winter. During the summer it regains the 20 feet when the

Washington

snows in the mountains start to melt. The lake does not freeze during the winter. Being such a large body of water, it maintains a fairly constant temperature which influences the temperatures of the surrounding land. The western part of the lake has a shoreline dominated with high mountains, steep cliffs and beautiful forests. As one moves "down lake" this pattern gives way to rolling hills with orchards and delightful little towns.

Chelan is located a reasonable distant from the larger urban areas in the state of Washington. Seattle is 166 miles, Spokane is 146 miles and Wenatchee is 37 miles to the south. The roads are good and the travel time is reasonable for shopping, business trips, and entertainment.

Summary: Chelan is one of the more attractive areas in the Northwest. Real estate is fairly expensive but the environment is beyond description. There are numerous outdoor activities in which to engage. The civic services are adequate and medical facilities are close at hand. This is a magnificent place to live. It has the beautiful blue lake, tree studded mountains, clear skies, flowering orchards and four distinct seasons. Chelan is a definite place for further investigation.

Wenatchee (25,000 Pop.)

The Wenatchee Valley is a beautiful fruit growing area in north central Washington. To the west are the forest-covered, snow-capped Cascade Mountains and to the east a high plateau where the fields of grain ripen in the warm eastern Washington sunshine. The valley supports a population of approximately 49,000 with the city of Wenatchee accounting for more than half of the residents. Wenatchee is located on the "mighty" Columbia and Wenatchee rivers. It is looked upon by many Washingtonians as one of the best places to live. This view reinforces G. Scott Thomas' conclusions in his study of life in small American towns where he ranked Wenatchee 4th out of 219 towns studied.

Wenatchee's economy depends greatly on agriculture: fruit growing and processing, grains and livestock. Wenatchee is the apple capital of the state of Washington. More than 1/2

Washington

of the state's apple crop is produced in the Wenatchee Valley. More than 70% of the monetary production of the valley comes from agriculture. Other industries and business ventures, that aid in producing a very stable economy in Wenatchee, are the metals industry, power generation, regional health care services, retail enterprises and tourism. The cost of living, as with all of eastern Washington, is less expensive than is the case of the greater Seattle region.

Prices for homes in the Wenatchee area have been climbing in recent years but they still remain very reasonable when compared to western Washington and many of the larger western United States urban areas. A new three bedroom/ two bath home can be purchased for $120,000. Lots can run as low as $30,000 and small acreages, although scarce and some distance from town, will start in the mid $100,000 range. Some very fine larger homes are available, many with truly wonderful territorial views. These homes start in the high $100,000s and go up to the $300,000s. Both East Wenatchee and Wenatchee have outstanding view locations.

Wenatchee provides regional health care for a four county area. The medical services employ approximately 2,000 people. The hospital, Central Washington Hospital, is a 176 bed facility employing a staff of 900. It provides a comprehensive health care program for both physical and mental needs. This facility is supported by a number of clinics specializing in such fields as cancer, eye and ear and general health Also, Wenatchee has a number of skilled nursing facilities, personal care centers and retirement villages. Like any city of this size, the police and fire departments are manned by professionals and the 911 system is available.

A real plus with Wenatchee, as well as Chelan and a portion of Douglas County, is the free Link bus service which connects a number of cities and provides intercity transportation for the residents. Panghorn Memorial Airport provides for commuter air transport to the larger airports of Spokane and Seattle. Wenatchee's location in north central Washington, where there are a number of hydroelectric dams, makes electricity inexpensive.

There are two school districts in the Wenatchee area. The Eastmont School District serves the area in and around

Washington

East Wenatchee and the Wenatchee District provides service to the city and surrounding area. Between the two, there are over 10,000 pupils, with Eastmont being the smallest district. Both districts offer a comprehensive educational program and both have very good reputations within the state.

Higher education is provided by Wenatchee Valley Community College. This institution not only offers an academic program but also has a fine vocational-technical program. Tree fruit production and nursing programs are especially strong at Wenatchee Valley Community College. Upper division and graduate level courses are provided by Central Washington and Washington State universities.

As for cultural opportunities, the city is large enough to support some very fine organizations. There is a conference center in Wenatchee which can provide for performing arts productions. Local musical groups consist of the British Brass Band, Wenatchee Valley Symphony, Appola Men's Choir, Appleaires Women's Chorus, Columbia Flute Society, Community Concert and the Big Bands of the 50's.

When it comes to theater performance, Wenatchee can boast of the Music Theatre of Wenatchee, Wenatchee Youth Theatre, Wenatchee Civic Ballet and the Mission Creek Players. A unique feature of the Wenatchee area is the Wenatchee Youth Circus. This is a non-animal circus and is not something a person would envision to be offered in Wenatchee, Washington, Florida perhaps, but not in Wenatchee.

Recreation opportunities are numerous. If one likes to boat, fish, water ski or wind surf there are huge lakes behind the power dams all up and down the Columbia. For the golf enthusiasts, there are six 18 hole courses within a short distance from Wenatchee. The Wenatchee River affords a person the thrill of shooting rapids (experienced guides are a necessity). Deer and elk hunting is good in the nearby mountains. Bird hunting in the valley and the plateau east of Wenatchee is great. The mountains offer summer hiking, camping, backpacking and trail riding. In the winter, there is great downhill skiing at Mission Ridge, which is just 12 miles from downtown. Cross country skiing, snowshoeing and snowmobiling is also available in the Wenatchee area. If one likes to ice skate or play hockey, the city has two ice rinks available.

Washington

Wenatchee is in the center of the state of Washington. Seattle is 138 miles to the west and Spokane is 165 miles to the east. The Canadian border is 145 miles to the north and the Oregon border is 185 miles to the south.

Summary: After visiting Wenatchee, it is not hard to figure out why it is a very popular place to live or visit. The economy is stable, the cost of living is reasonable, real estate is not expensive, health care is good and there are numerous cultural and recreational opportunities. There are four distinct seasons. It is a much drier climate than one will find on the west side of the Cascades. The sun shines most of the year, and the annual snowfall is tolerable.

Okanogan County
Omak and Okanogan (6,200 Pop.)

One of the last areas in the state of Washington to be discovered is the unspoiled wonderland of Okanogan County. The county has over 5,000 square miles with a density of 6 people per square mile. For the purpose of this report, only the valley along the Okanogan River will be discussed. This valley is bordered on the west by the Cascade Mountains with peaks towering over 8,000 ft. To the east of the valley are highlands with rolling hills, ranches and some lesser peaks ranging from 5,000 to 6,000 feet in height. The valley is dominated by the Okanogan River which flows south to join the Columbia River near Brewster. The valley is capped by the Canadian border and beautiful Lake Osoyoos. The weather is not unlike that of Wenatchee. Rain is limited to around 10 inches annually and the snow will occur mostly in December through February and will annually average 30 inches.

The main centers of population are Omak and Okanogan. Omak is the commercial center with Okanogan being the governmental center. The towns are right next door to each other and have a combined population of about 6,200 residents.

The main contributors to the economic life of the communities are wood products, tree fruit (apples) and livestock. Wood products and governmental operations employ the bulk

Washington

of the labor force. Wood products and agricultural enterprises create a seasonal labor market.

Real estate is about as reasonable as one will find in the state of Washington. This area is being discovered and the demand for small plots of land is heavy. One would think that such plots would be plentiful but this is not the case. Much of the land is considered valuable farm land. The farmers are not anxious to see the farms broken up into smaller plots when the land, as it is, is producing a good return. Regulations and the cost of short platting are also inhibitors to forming small parcels. If small parcels (5 -15 acres) with reasonable homes can be found they can be purchased for $150,000 and up. Good homes in town can be found in the low $100,000. "Fixers" have become popular and can be purchased for a very reasonable price. The thing to remember is that the market is a "sellers" market, so it pays to look around and get to know the housing prices in the community. Property taxes are relatively low, ranging from $15 to $17 per $1000 of assess valuation.

Omak and Okanogan both rely upon volunteers for fire services. These two towns cooperate with each other regarding fire service needs. Omak maintains a police department while Okanogan relies upon the Okanogan Sheriff's Office. Omak has a 44 bed hospital which is capable of providing comprehensive medical services. For cases that are beyond their capabilities they rely upon Central Washington Hospital in Wenatchee or the larger facilities located in Seattle or Spokane.

There are two public school districts which serve approximately 3,000 youths - 1/3 by Okanogan and the rest by Omak's school district. Wenatchee Valley Community College has a north campus located in Omak. Washington State University provides four year and extension programs at the North Campus facility. Omak also has a small private 4 year institution called Heritage College. This college focuses on interdisciplinary studies and education. Both towns have airports. Omak has the most sophisticated facility, with a 4,600 foot paved runway, lights and instrument approach capability.

The Okanogan country has a rich history in precious metals. Gold can still be found by the skilled prospector. Gold and silver rushes are history and only a number of "ghost" towns remain. These are located in the highlands to the east of the valley. Wauconda is one of these towns. It was founded in 1898 and, at its peak, it had a population of 335, three hotels, four saloons, a store, boarding house and a blacksmith shop. All that remains is the store. These towns draw a lot of curious travelers and are a great reminder of what the "old west" looked like.

The focus of the Omak-Okanogan area is really pointed toward the active outdoors life. There are rodeos, the most famous being the Omak Stampede with its world famous Suicide Race. The rodeo is first class and the Suicide Race is thrilling. During the race, horse and rider gallop full-tilt down a very steep incline into the river, swim across and end in the rodeo arena. It is a miracle that more horses and riders are not injured, which is a tribute to the horses and their expert riders. Almost every community in the area has some kind of rodeo. Tonasket, a small town above Omak, has a Pony Express Friendship Ride which carries the mail in a 10 hour period to Princeton, British Columbia, a ride of approximately 90 miles.

There are all sorts of things to do in this wonderland. In the winter there is downhill skiing at Loup Loup or Sitzmark, snowshoeing, cross country skiing, snowmobiling, ice fishing at Conconully Lake, ice skating, and fishing for the wary Steelhead. In the spring and summer one can focus on fishing (237 lakes), golf, "off-roading", rodeos, swimming, boating, river rafting, water skiing, hiking and backpacking. In the fall, hunting is good, fishing is still around, hot air balloons start to appear more often, and bird watching is enjoyable.

As for cultural pursuits, the 560 seat Performing Arts Center brings entertainment and educational programs to the residents of Omak and Okanogan and the surrounding countryside. The North Campus also adds to the cultural and educational opportunities. There are a number of museums in the Valley, each bringing the observer reminders of the past. The Colville Indian Reservation brings the nearby communities an awareness of the rich past of the Native American. Of course, just 100 miles to the south is Wenatchee which augments the entertainment and cultural activities of the Okanogan Valley resident.

Washington

Summary: This area is definitely for those who want a more rural environment with plenty of outdoor activity. If one is interested in farming or livestock, then this is a great place. The medical facilities and other services are adequate. Real estate is reasonable. It is a small community and, as such, it doesn't have a lot of work available for new residents. The valley seems to be ideally suited for the person who has some financial independence, wants the outdoor life, a little land , and a slower pace.

Northeastern Washington

This part of Washington is mountainous and fairly dry. The dome-like mountains are covered with forests of pine, fir, larch and the beautiful aspen. The mountain ranges consist of the Selkirk Range to the east and the Kettle Falls Range to the west. The valleys have grassy meadows and small streams which are lined with willow and cottonwood. This part of Washington is truly a beautiful place. It is majestic in scope and in the fall the leaves and needles present a gorgeous tapestry of golds, reds, oranges and greens. It is breathtaking.

Here Washington is remote and is not highly populated. The cities are small and few. This is one of the places in Washington where small and large ranches are numerous. Much of the land reminds one of the landscape that was pictured on the TV show that was called *"Bonanza."*

The economy is driven by the timber industry, cattle, mining and fruit growing. The mountains gave up their gold during a strike in the late 19th century but gold is still being extracted by persevering prospectors and miners. Timber is by far the biggest cash crop.

Tourism is also important to the economy. Lake Roosevelt, the lake created by the Grand Coulee Dam in the 1930s, brings a large number of visitors to this area. It is the largest lake in Washington, stretching over 151 miles to the Canadian border and beyond. This huge lake provides opportunities for great fishing and boating. Camping, hiking and hunting are all favorite activities for the natives and visitors alike.

Washington

Northeastern Washington has a definite four season climate. In the summers it is dry and warm. The winters are snowy and cold. The saving grace, as far as climate conditions go, is the humidity is low.

Spokane is the largest metropolitan area for this region. It serves as the retail and commercial center for the region. The smaller communities rely upon the Spokane hospitals to handle severe medical cases that require specialized care. Spokane International Airport serves the region with national and international air transportation.

Only one community was selected for discussion. Colville is one of the larger communities in the region. Except for size, it is typical of many of the smaller communities.

Colville (5,000 Pop.)

Colville is a small community located in the northeastern corner of Washington. It is surrounded by rugged mountains, forests of Douglas fir, larch, and Ponderosa pines. It is the largest city in Stevens County and is the county seat. This area is well known for a large number of lakes, 306 to be exact. The largest lake is Lake Roosevelt which is a 151 mile long lake created by the Grand Coulee Dam.

Timber and wood products are important economic drivers for this region. Agriculture and tourism are also important. Lake Roosevelt and the mountains accommodate many tourists during the summer. Colville, like many county seats, has a number of governmental agencies which add to the economic stability of the community.

Real estate prices are reasonable. The taxes are relatively low. A newer three bedroom/ two bath home can be purchased for as little as $115,000. Small ranchettes can be found in the mid $100,000 range. Larger spreads can be purchased in the $200,000 range and up. For example, a 128 acre ranch with a house, shop, hay barn, equipment and cattle was listed for $250,000 about the price of a 2000 square foot home in the Seattle area. So, if it is country living a person wants, Colville is a good place to look.

Mount Carmel Hospital is small but capable of handling most cases. Those medical situations that require some

Washington

type of specialized service can receive it in Spokane, just 65 mile to the south. Police and fire protection is good and 911 is available.

The public schools have an enrollment of 2,550. Their secondary program has been recognized as one of the best in Washington. The newer 14 million dollar high school is one of the outstanding features of the community. Besides providing a wonderful environment for the educational program, it provides the community with a first-rate performing arts center. Spokane's community colleges have satellite programs which are enjoyed by the citizens of the community. There are four universities and colleges within 150 miles of Colville.

The local airport is small. It has a 2,400 foot runway and it handles private and corporate aircraft. For national and international flight connections the citizen must go to the Spokane International Airport—65 miles to the south.

The summer days are hot and dry with cool nights. The winters can get very cold and snow is a frequent visitor. The falls are glorious with color, frosty morning, warm afternoons and cool evenings. Springs are welcome in this neck of the woods. The winters are hard and the first warmth of spring is greatly appreciated.

Much of the entertainment and cultural events spring from the schools. The performing arts facility at the high school provides an excellent atmosphere for school and community cultural and entertainment events. Close by Kettle Falls has a local theater group that puts on exceptional productions at the R.F. Woodland Theater.

Colville thinks a great deal of its past. There are a number of historic sites maintained by the citizens. One of the most outstanding is the Keller House. This is a splendid home built in the early 1900s and is maintained as a National Historical Site. The Christmas holidays are a celebration time for the town folks. The Keller House is brightly decorated and open for visitors. Something unique to Colville during this holiday season is the mule drawn trolley which takes visitors for rides. It is one of the fun things to which the natives and visitors look forward.

For fun and excitement one only has to take part in the Rendezvous activities such as the car show, three on three bas-

Washington

ketball, the egg toss and other games and activities. By the way, if one can beat a 92 foot egg toss it is worth $500. Oh yes, what would Colville be without its rodeo and regional fair?

Spokane, being relatively close, provides many cultural and entertainment opportunities for the citizens of Colville. Shopping trips to the city usually turn out to be a delightful all day affair.

Colville is mountain, forest, lake and river country. Consequently, the outdoors recreational activities revolve around these natural features. Hunting for big game is popular in the fall with fishing left for the warmer months.

Lake Roosevelt and the hundreds of lesser lakes provide abundant opportunities for boating and fishing. There are 23 species of fish available in this section of Washington.

The mountains provide an environment that lends itself to hiking, backpacking, climbing, horseback riding, camping, snowmobiling, and cross country skiing. Downhill skiing requires some travel. Latitude 49, a skiing facility, is relatively close and the Idaho destination resort of Schweitzer is within striking distance.

Colville is not far from Spokane, about 1 1/2 hours. Seattle is considerably farther, 353 miles and the Canadian border is approximately 35 miles.

Summary: Colville is a neat, clean, little town in northeastern Washington. The people are hard working and take pride in their community. The economy is dependent on timber, agriculture and tourism. Real estate prices are reasonable and there are a number of larger pieces of land available. The schools are good and extension classes for higher education are available. Cultural and entertainment activities benefit from the presence of a nice performing arts center, historical interests, and the closeness of Spokane for major events. The town has adequate protection services and a good hospital. Recreations is oriented toward the mountains and lakes.

Colville strikes one as a safe place for long walks on a warm summer evening, chatting with neighbors, fishing on a calm lake in the early morning mist, hunting for the big buck, growing a prize winning garden, taking part in the annual Rendezvous egg toss and taking an occasional trip to Spokane to take in a play or shop for a gift for the wife or husband. It is a calm place, a place where one can catch their breath.

Southeastern Washington

Washington is a state that has many geological faces. Southeastern Washington is one of these many faces. The area of focus in this discussion will be the Walla Walla Valley which epitomizes much of southeastern Washington. This region can best be described as the territory that is bounded on the north by the awesome Snake River, on the west by the mighty Columbia, to the south by the Oregon border and to the east by Idaho. This is a region with rolling hills, small streams, few trees, great fields of golden grains, large farms and some beautiful mountains to the southeast.

The Walla Walla Valley is located in the southern central portion of this larger region. In this part of Washington agriculture is what turns the economic wheel. There is some manufacturing but it is not pervasive. Wood products are also part of the economy.

The colleges and medical services, along with commercial interest, pretty well sum up the economic picture of this region.

Walla Walla, the largest city in this region, serves as the cultural, entertainment, medical and commercial center.

Real estate is reasonable throughout the region. Walla Walla has the highest prices but even these are reasonable.

The bulk of the population is located in three cities, Walla Walla, College Place and Clarkston. (Clarkston will not be part of this discussion. It will be considered along with Lewiston, Idaho in another section.) (Milton Freewater, although in Oregon, is right on the border and will be discussed as part of the Walla Walla Valley).

The public schools in Washington are good and that goes for this region. There are three colleges located in the valley.

The focus of much of the recreational activities is on the outdoors. The colleges, along with civic efforts, provide opportunities to enjoy dramatic and musical productions, art

Washington

and lecture series. The traditional rodeos, fairs and festivals also flourish.

The summers are usually hot and dry and the winters are cold, rainy and snowy. It is a region that definitely has four seasons and the springs and falls are quite pleasant.

There is a wind that is called a "Chinook". It comes in often after a cold spell and melts the snow and ice. This wind seems to reenergize the whole community. This is one of the things that one always remembers with great fondness.

Walla Walla (26,500 Pop.), College Place (6,500 Pop.), and Milton Freewater, Oregon (5,700 Pop.)

Walla Walla, so the story goes, is the town they liked so well they named it twice. The Indians referred to the valley as the land of "many waters". It is the place where Marcus Whitman, the famous missionary, established his mission.

The town is located in a valley that is 20 miles east of the Columbia River. Walla Walla, College Place and Milton Freewater, all share this wonderful valley. To the southeast of the valley are the Blue Mountains. They are relatively low but beautiful mountains often cloaked in a blue-like haze.

The city of Walla Walla with it giant deciduous trees, wide streets and large framed houses reminds one of the towns of the East and Midwest. College Place has some of the same qualities and Milton Freewater presents a community that reflects its agrarian interests.

The economy of the valley is oriented toward agriculture and food processing. Wheat is one of the major cash crops. Peas are still an important crop in the area and fruits provide another source of revenue. The famous Walla Walla Sweet Onions are grown here. Wine is starting to get some notice. Walla Walla is also famous for the state penitentiary, another major employer of the area.

Real estate is reasonable in Walla Walla and in College Place. Property in Milton Freewater is even more reasonable. A nice three bedroom/ two bath home in Walla Walla will cost in the low $100,000s. In Milton Freewater a similar home might cost in the neighborhood of $90,000. College Place

Washington

would also be less expensive than Walla Walla. Milton Freewater and College Place are becoming suburban communities for Walla Walla. View properties in Walla Walla are available in the high $100,000s and up. There are a number of developments that are putting up custom and spec homes that range in the $200,000s and up. If one is interested in grand homes with big yards on beautifully treed streets, then Walla Walla has a number of possibilities.

Walla Walla is large enough to provide all the services that a modern city needs. The police and fire departments are all paid professions. 911 is available and the hospitals, there are three, are first class. St. Mary's Hospital (142 beds) is a regional hospital for this part of southeastern Washington and northeastern Oregon. A smaller hospital, Walla Walla General (72) is also available. The Veterans' Hospital (150 beds) is located between Walla Walla and College Place.

The Walla Walla School District has an enrollment of 8,800 students. This is an enrollment that will allow a school district to provide a comprehensive program. The district is recognized as one of the outstanding districts in the state. The staff development program has received national recognition. College Place provides for elementary and middle school education, with the high school students going to Walla Walla for their schooling. Milton Freewater has a small consolidated school district of 1,800 students.

Post high school education for the area is provided by Whitman College, Walla Walla College and Walla Walla Community College. These are all fine colleges. Whitman College is recognized as one of the most outstanding liberal arts college in the United States. It is the nearest thing to the small eastern liberal arts college that one will find in the West. Walla Walla College is a small college with a fine program. The college is supported by the Seven Day Adventists. Walla Walla Community College is a state institution providing a 2 year degree program.

These institutions add to the cultural and entertainment opportunities for the three communities. There is a broad range of cultural events from which to choose, e.g., the Walla Walla Symphony (the oldest continuous run for a symphony west of the Mississippi), Cordiner Hall, at Whitman, which seats 1,500 and provides a number of programs, drama at the Harper Joy Theater at Whitman, the Whitman Arts and Lecture Series, Walla Walla College Lyceum Series, and Walla Walla Community Concerts.

In addition, the community enjoys other events like the Walla Walla Balloon Stampede, Wings over Walla Walla, and the Walla Walla Sweet Onion Harvest Festivals. Each of the smaller communities have there own festivals, like Milton Freewater's Muddy Frogwater Festival—it's great fun.

Recreation opportunities abound. The mountains provide downhill skiing opportunities at Bluewood, Spout Springs and Anthony Lakes. Snowmobiling, cross country skiing are also available in the mountain and foothills. Elk and deer hunting in the "Blues" is big in the fall. In the warmer months fishing, golf, hiking, and camping are favorites. Boating and water skiing at the Columbia River is available.

Walla Walla and the surrounding area is self-sufficient. The area is some 240 miles from Portland, 158 from Spokane and 262 miles to Seattle.

Summary: This is a very nice area. The cost of living is relative low, the towns provide good services. Education is valued in the community as witnessed by the quality of the school districts and the colleges. It is rare to find small rural areas with three fine colleges. Real estate is reasonable, with Milton Freewater and College Place offering the least expensive housing. Culturally, this area has some wonderful events and the recreation is on par with much of the Northwest. Walla Walla comes very close to those small communities one finds in the East and Midwest. It can provide a person a very wholesome environment in which to raise children and/or retire.

Oregon Map

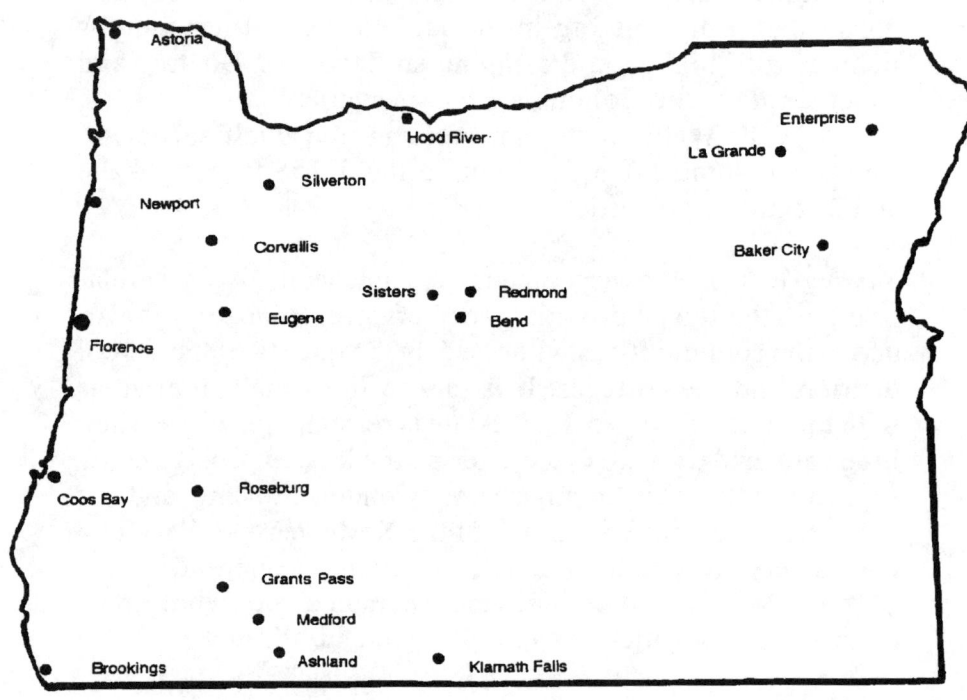

OREGON (3,086,000 Pop.)

Oregon, like Washington, is a land of contrasts. The high snow-capped Cascade Mountains separate the eastern and western regions. The eastern part of the state has high desert with its sage brush and juniper trees, deep canyons, wild rivers, pine forest and rolling hills with their golden grains. In the west one finds the beautiful Willamette Valley with its fertile fields, cool streams, neat farms, small towns, industry, large cities and most of the state's population. Separating the valley from the coast are the low Coast Range Mountains. The coast is a grand place with great headlands, jutting rock formations, great winter storms and lazy beautiful summer days.

The people of Oregon, like most Westerners, are open and warm. They have great pride their state and love its natural beauty. This is a state where rugged individualism is alive and well.

Eastern Oregon's summer weather is drier and warmer than western Oregon's. One hundred degree days are not unusual. The nights are generally cool. Winters will have snow and an occasional day of below zero temperatures. The mountains receive large amounts of snow during the winters.

Western Oregon has a mild climate. The summers rarely get days in the 90's or 100's. The exception to this will be in the inland valleys in southwestern Oregon. The winters in western Oregon are generally mild. Low temperatures run in the 30 - 50 degree range. Rain is a frequent visitor and cloudy days are common. Snow is generally reserved for the mountains. If snow does fall in the valleys, it is short-lived.

Oregon has some features, besides its beauty and grandeur, that are outstanding. The cost of living is one of the lowest in the nation. It has no sales tax, no motor vehicle excise tax, no business and occupation tax and no real estate transfer tax, and the local property tax rate is $15 per $1000 of assessed value. Oregon does have an income tax. For a joint return the maximum marginal rate is 9% of taxable income in excess of $10,000. Oregon ranked eighth lowest in state taxes in the United States (*Kiplinger's Personal Finance Magazine*, August 1995, pp. 58-59).

Oregon

The largest industries are forest products, agriculture, and tourism. High-tech is gaining strength in the state. Oregon's electricity rates are among the lowest in the nation.

For a West coast state, real estate prices are generally reasonable. As one would expect the smaller communities have the lowest real estate prices. There are a few exceptions to this statement, for example, Sisters, Bend and Ashland. The larger communities like Eugene and Portland will have higher housing prices.

Where medical accommodations are concerned, specifics will be given as we discuss individual communities. There are four major medical centers in Oregon: Portland, Eugene, Medford and Bend. Of course, each community has taken steps to provide for routine medical care.

The state has an outstanding system of higher education. The high school students consistently earn the second highest SAT scores in the nation.

Culturally, Oregon is very well served. Portland provides an expansive menu of cultural, entertainment and sport activities. Cities like Eugene, Corvallis, Salem, Medford, Ashland, Newport, Klamath Falls and Bend all provide great cultural and entertainment opportunities. The smaller communities have their own unique rodeos, fairs and festivals. People are willing to drive miles to larger cities to enjoy what is offered in the way of cultural and entertainment opportunities.

Recreationally, Oregon, like the rest of the Pacific Northwest, focuses on outdoor activities. It does not matter whether a person is in the east or west of Oregon, the number of outdoor recreational opportunities will boggle the mind.

Let us now turn our attention to some specific parts of the state. For the purpose of presentation we have divided Oregon into a number of geographical regions (Oregon Coast, Willamette Valley, Umpqua and Rogue Valleys, Central Oregon, and Northeastern Oregon).

Oregon Coast

The Oregon coast is spectacular. It is one of the most beautiful coast lines of America. It has huge headlands that jut out into the sea and provide for some beautiful crescent shaped beaches. Monolith-like rocks rise up from the sea all along the coast. Sizable rivers flow down from the Coast and Siuslaw mountain ranges to join the vast Pacific on the southern coast. Here the shoreline becomes increasingly rugged.

This is an area that owes much of its prosperity to the forests and the sea. Forest products, although somewhat restrained by the spotted owl preservation situation, are still a major industrial force. Fishing is also having some difficulties. Fishing is still going on but the beautiful sleek salmon, so much prized, has become more and more scarce. Government regulations, dams, pollution and mismanagement have all accounted for making the Oregon coast fisherman's life more difficult. Because of the hard times for the forest and fishing industries, there has been considerable attention paid to retraining people. This has allowed the coast of hold down unemployment more than one might expect. A number of communities visited by the author, gave evidence of the importance they were placing on strategic economic planning for their communities.

Tourism has always been important to the Oregon coast's economy and now it is even more important. Another growth industry, albeit small, is the research and development operations in marine environments and seafood processing.

The climate is very similar all along the coast. The one major exception is the Brookings area and more will be said about the "Banana Belt" when we specifically discuss Brookings. Sixty inches of rain is about par for most of the coast. Rain is heaviest in the late fall and winter months. It is during this time that one experiences the leaden skies associated with a marine climate. Many people use the rainy weather as an opportune time to enjoy the solitude and to think and prepare themselves for the busier times.

One of the more interesting times is when the exhilarating winter storms blow in off the great Pacific Ocean. The ocean turns into a giant maelstrom sending crushing waves against the rugged coast with its mighty headlands. It is awesome to stand in the grip of these storms and feel the full fury of Mother Nature as she hurls her silvered sprayed waves and mighty wind against you. Often after the storm is spent and

Oregon

moves on inland, the coast is rewarded with clearing skies, brilliant sunshine and crystal-clear panoramic views.

Even though the winter months have their big storms, snow is rare on the coast. As winter passes, the summers become comfortably warm with normal temperatures in the 60s and 70s and perhaps, with some 80s on rare occasions.

The Oregon coast is a wonderful place for kites, marine life investigations, beach combing, playing in the surf, building sand castles, whale watching, riding dune buggies, camping, hiking, fishing, hunting, history of the area and shopping. It is definitely a place for the family.

The coast has a history of being treacherous for ships. The river bars and rocky coast have, over the years, provided many stories of ships being destroyed by the giant Pacific storms. This is one of the reasons for the large number of historical lighthouses. These life saving beacons have warned many mariners of the dangerous Oregon coast.

The majority of the coastal rivers meet the mighty Pacific head on, which results in dangerous bar activity. The U.S. Coast Guard is in strong evidence at many of the more dangerous bars. The one river that does not have this bar problem is the Chetco River at Brooking.

Highway 101 runs the full length of the Oregon coast. It is a highway that is, for the most part, in very good repair. There are at least nine highways that cross the mountains to the Willamette Valley. Most of them are in the northern three quarters of the coast.

Oregon has a public beach law. Only a very small portion of the Oregon coast is closed to the public. This allows for a great number of state parks along the Oregon coast. There are many splendid beaches - beaches that are long, wide and clean. One of the natural marvels of the Oregon coast is the great sand dunes that appear on the coast between Florence and Coos Bay, to the south. These dunes sometimes reach the height of 300 plus feet.

Real estate prices are reasonable all up and down the coast, that is, if you are use to West coast prices. If a person comes from the Midwest or southern states, then the prices might seem a bit high. Easterners will probably find the prices

Oregon

about the same or slightly lower. One thing for sure is prices and availability are not improving for the buyer.

The coast's population is growing, which is true for all of Oregon. With this growth, competition for good home sites is increasing which results in the escalation of prices. Keep in mind what is really being purchased is a "way of life". If one is looking for a slower pace, natural beauty and friendly people, you will have to go a long way to beat Oregon's coast.

The following communities to be discussed are Astoria, Newport, Florence, Coos Bay and Brookings.

Astoria (10,069)

Three rivers, the "mighty Columbia", the Young and the Lewis and Clark meet at Astoria, the second largest city on the Oregon coast. This little community is located at the mouth of the Columbia and has survived, for many years, the awesome effects of river water and ocean wind.

The town's economy relies heavily on wood products and fishing. Tourism is also an important economic contributor.

Tongue Point Job Corp Center is located in Astoria. This center concentrates on providing training programs for young folks with a low income background. In addition, the Management Training Corporation is located there providing training and placement services for Clatsop County employers and residents. There is also a new training center being developed which will deal with the marine environment and maritime matters.

Much of Astoria is located on high hills which run along the Columbia. The view of marine traffic going up the Columbia and out to the Pacific is magnificent. There are any number of older Victorian style homes on the Astoria hillsides. Some have been renovated and are exceptional. Other homes are just waiting to be restored.

Real estate in Astoria and the nearby Warrenton area is very reasonable. A three bedroom/two bath home can be found from $90,000 and up. Unlike a number of communities on the Oregon coast, Astoria has a good supply of homes and lots.

Oregon

Full-time police and fire services are provided. Astoria has an airport that serves the U.S. Coast Guard as well as private and commercial aircraft. The town has the largest Coast Guard facility between the Puget Sound and San Francisco. The 911 emergency system exists and the average response time for the ambulance service is 4 minutes. The Columbia Memorial Hospital is a 49 bed acute care facility and was built in 1977. For the more complicated medical procedures, the Portland hospitals are available.

The public schools are good and Clatsop Community College provides a 2-year program. The University of Oregon, Oregon State University, and Portland State University provide extension services to the community.

The Clatsop Community College provides the community with a performing arts center. In addition, the Astor Street Opry Company, a summer theater group, is alive and well. Astoria has a Scandinavian heritage with many parts of the town and surrounding countryside tagged with Scandinavian names. Each year the annual Scandinavian Festival is held. Besides this festival, the Astoria area has eight other festive occasions, e.g. Oregon Dixieland Jubilee, a county fair, and the Astoria Regatta.

Because of Astoria's rich historical past, the community has two museums, one is an outstanding maritime collection and the other is a general historical collection. More recent history is to be found at Fort Stevens, which was the recipient of a Japanese submarine shelling in 1942. This is reported to be the first time since the War of 1812 that a foreign country has shelled the continental United States.

The Columbia River is very broad at its mouth and the Astoria - Megler Bridge, which is 4.1 miles long, gives the visitor some idea of the river's width. This bridge has the distinction of being the longest continuous tress span in the world.

The Columbia, at its mouth, is famous for it hazardous bar conditions. Large ships require a pilot to take them across the bar and up or down the river. There have been times when ships and boats have had to wait outside the bar until it settled down. There have been many a sport fisherman to lose their breakfast crossing that bar.

Once across the bar, barring a Pacific storm, the water is relativity calm. The shipping traffic is usually headed up river to Longview, Washington or Portland, Oregon. Barge traffic is heavy on the Columbia and Snake River system up as far as Lewiston, Idaho. From that point on the dams do not allow barge traffic.

Boating is big in Astoria. For the sailor, there are mooring basins at Astoria, Warrenton and Hammond, which lease by the day, month or year. Of course, sailing on the Columbia is fabulous.

The rivers, ocean and lakes provide plenty of fishing opportunities to catch the "big one". If you are a hunter, then there are elk, deer, bear and waterfowl to tax your skills.

Astoria is 95 miles from Portland via Highway 30. The highway is well maintained and very picturesque with its rolling forested hills and river views. The road generally follows the Columbia River to its confluence with the Willamette River at Portland.

Summary: The town is stable and has lots of activities in which people can get involved. Real estate opportunities, the Victorian homes, the excitement of the river and its traffic, and its proximity to Portland are all good points for considering Astoria. The fresh air, a warm fire and a hot cup of coffee makes one more tolerant of the winter weather. The summers are very nice. For fisher persons, hunters, boaters, antique shoppers and folks who just want a simpler lifestyle, Astoria is definitely worth a look-see.

Newport (9,000 Pop.)

Newport is a town that appears to have great vitality. *Pacific Northwest Magazine,* in the early 1990's, included it in an article called "Paradise Found: 12 Great Towns You Could Call Home".

Newport is a commercial town. The business of the town is business. It has a four phase economy - fishing, wood products, tourism and research and development. This four pronged economy provides stability to the community.

Oregon

The Hatfield Marine Science Center is located in Newport as are the Environmental Protection Laboratory and Oregon Coast Aquarium. NOAA (National Oceanic Atmospheric Administration) is conducting studies on underwater thermal activity off the Oregon coast and is based at Newport. The science orientation of the above facilities brings many graduate students and visiting scientists to the area. Newport, also, houses one of the largest commercial fishing fleets in Oregon.

Shopping is good in Newport. The community is large enough to support a sizable retail business community. There are a number of shopping centers. The "old town", down by the harbor, is fascinating and has many places where a person can shop and get a fine meal—seafood, of course.

Real estate is similar to what one would expect to pay on this section of the coast. A newer three bedroom/two bath home without a view would go for about $165,000. The same home with a view would be in the neighborhood of $200,000 plus. Beachfront homes sell in the range of $300,000 to $400,000. Of course, condos are somewhat less expensive. Southshore, an upscale development, is located a short distance south of Newport. The prices in this development run from $180,000 to $350,000 and up. One should be aware that prices have been going up all along the Oregon coast, which probably comes as no surprise to most of us.

Health care in Newport is very good. The Pacific Communities Hospital has been serving the community since the early fifties and can handle most of the required medical services. Like so many of the Oregon coast communities, they can rely on air ambulance service to take patients with very serious problems to the larger regional hospitals of the Willamette Valley. The community has a 911 emergency system.

Professional police and fire services are provided. The area has a good airport that can handle instrument landing - very handy in an area that has fog. Portland provides national and international air service.

The public school program is provided by the Lincoln County School District. This district has an enrollment of approximately 7,000 students. It is a district of 17 schools and provides a comprehensive program which serves 6 communi-

Oregon

ties. Newport is also home to the Oregon Coast Community College which provides programs in technical training and college prep. Oregon State University provides extension classes in the Newport area.

The citizens take an active role in shaping the community's amenities. The folks of Newport, in both age and spirit, are relatively young. The Performing Arts Center provides the community with many fine art opportunity. Work is going on to develop an artist facility called "Thundering Seas". This is a facility that will feature jewelry, woods and metals. The Visual Arts Center exhibits the works of visiting and local artists. To mention a few of the other outstanding features of the cultural environment: Newport has three dance groups, several theater groups, a chamber orchestra and a 400 seat performance theater. In addition to the above, there are several annual festivals dealing with music and film. It is a place where everyone, no matter their age or taste, can find something for themselves.

Recreationally, Newport is able to provide a vast array of activities. The sea provides opportunities for fishing and boating. One can hike miles on a beautiful sea coast. The mountains and rivers have good hunting and fishing. Hiking and camping are favorite pursuits of many of the folks in Newport. With the college and other amenities of the town, there are many opportunities to enjoy first-class entertainment.

Newport has excellent proximity to the larger urban communities of the Willamette Valley. Portland is 114 and Eugene is 92 miles from Newport.

Summary: The community has a vigorous business atmosphere, impressive cultural facilities and good real estate opportunities. It has good schools, a fine hospital and professional civic services. Digby Cook, a resident of Newport, who has lived and traveled all over the world, chose Newport as a good place to settle and go into business. A number of people come to Newport to visit and come back to stay. It is a place that has a vitality and beauty that appeals to many looking for a "home".

Oregon

Florence (5,700 Pop.)

Florence, an attractive community, is made even more appealing by the beautiful nearby lakes, the Siuslaw River and the great ocean which resides at its doorstep. The forested Coast Range mountains provide a gorgeous backdrop for this town, the lakes, the river and the ocean.

Like most of the Oregon coast towns, Florence relies on the forest, tourism and the ocean for its living. This community is definitely looking for ways to diversify its economic base. An economic development plan is underway which focuses on providing "family wage" jobs. The high-tech industry is of much interest to the planners.

To help the fishing industry, large artificial reefs are being developed offshore. These reefs provide habitat for the fish. Florence has a large tourist industry. The Oregon Dunes National Recreation Area is close by and draws hundreds of thousand tourist each year.

Real estate in Florence is similar to the north coast prices. A three bedroom/two bath home with no view sells for $75,000 to $160,000, with a view $200,000 and up, and on the coast $350,000 plus. One of the nice features of Florence is that there are four possible settings for a home. Heceta Beach, just slightly northwest of Florence, has beach orientations. Dunes City and other areas with lakes can provide wonderful lake orientations. One thing that makes the lake orientation desirable is the fact that it is quieter and the ocean mist and the salt is less of a problem. There is a city orientation and also there is the woods setting. Florence has a good inventory of new construction and many other real estate opportunities. The town is attractive to many retired people.

Florence has the essential services for a town its size. It has a good modern library, utility services, police and fire protection, public schools and a U.S. Coast Guard Station is located there. Lane Community College, in Eugene, provides extension services to the area. Hospital services are provided by the Peace Harbor Hospital. This hospital has a close working relationship with Sacred Heart General Hospital and Medical Center in Eugene. Sacred Heart is a regional hospital and handles the more critical cases from the region.

Eugene, the second largest city in Oregon, is 60 miles from Florence and not only does it augment the medical services of Florence but it supplies many of the cultural and entertainment amenities. Eugene is the home of the University of Oregon, the Hult Center, a performing arts center, and provides for big city shopping and other services. Florence is developing an all event center to provide more local cultural and entertainment opportunities.

The Florence area provides an outdoor recreation paradise. For the fisherman there is the river, the lakes and the ocean. Here a person can hook the mighty salmon, the hard to catch steelhead, the cutthroat trout, halibut, ling cod and snapper. The hunter can stalk elk, deer, bear, and try his/her luck with ducks and geese. The lakes provide fresh water swimming, boating and fishing. The mountains, beaches and dunes allow opportunities to hike. The 300 feet high dunes provide plenty of opportunities to try dune buggies, ride horses and swim at Honeyman State Park. If you like to ride a bike, then Florence is a grand place—few hills.

Summary: Florence can provide good shopping, cultural and entertainment opportunities. The schools, protection services and medical facilities are good. The close proximity of Eugene and its services makes Florence even more desirable. Recreational opportunities abound with the mountains, lakes, river and ocean. The Florence area provides a variety of environments for building which makes it unique among the coast communities. Real estate is reasonable and there appears to be sufficient availability. Florence is an attractive place and it might just be what a person is looking for in a community.

Coos Bay (15,000 Pop.)

This area is popularly referred to as the Bay Area, but is actually made up of three communities: Coos Bay, North Bend, and Charleston. The combined area has a population of over 31,000 with a service area of over 90,000. The Bay Area is the retail, cultural, medical and professional center of the southern Oregon coast.

Oregon

As one drives through the Bay Area on Highway 101, justice is not done to the community. This route takes a person through the industrial and shipping areas. These areas are certainly part of the economic lifeblood of the community but lack the attractiveness of some of the residential areas in the surrounding hills.

The economy of the Bay Area is dependent upon fishing, forest products and shipping. It hosts one of the world's leading forest products shipping ports. The community is certainly large enough to support almost any business venture and shopping opportunities are plentiful. Tourism is on the rise.

One finds a wide selection of real estate opportunities in the Bay Area. A new three bedroom/two bath home on a city lot sells for around $100,000. Ocean front lots go for $150,000 and up and view lots run between $40,000 and $50,000. A good view home costs $150,000 and up. The prices in the Bay Area are some of the lowest on the Oregon coast.

The health services are as good as one will find on the Oregon coast. The Bay Area Hospital has 172 beds and 85 physicians on staff. The hospital serves as a regional hospital for the southern Oregon coast. A 911 emergency system is also available. The ambulance service is staffed by EMT's (Emergency Medical Technicians) and paramedics. There is an air ambulance service capable of flying patients to any community west of the Mississippi.

The North Bend Municipal Airport provides good commercial connections. The U.S. Coast Guard is strongly represented in the Bay Area. Their primary mission is air and sea rescue and law enforcement.

As with the large majority of public school districts in the state of Oregon, the Bay Area schools are good. Higher education is represented by the Southeastern Oregon Community College and the University of Oregon Institute of Marine Biology at Charleston. Besides the local colleges, extension services are provided by private and other public four year institutions.

The weather is just a little different in the Bay Area - it is slightly warmer and has slightly less rain than the rest of the coast. The months of June, July, August, and September, with an average rainfall of about one inch per month, are very pleasant.. The annual average temperature ranges from 50 to 54 degrees.

Coos Bay has the only art museum on the Oregon coast. The fact is, there are only four art museums in all of Oregon. There are three little theater groups in the area and they are quite capable of putting on first class productions. The Oregon Coast Music Association sponsors the annual Oregon Coast Music Festival in the month of July. Of course, the presence of a community college also adds greatly to the cultural climate of the area.

For the outdoors person, the Bay Area has everything that is available in the other communities along the coast. Golf is more prevalent here than in some of the other communities. Don't forget the spectacular and beautiful parks that are in the Bay Area vicinity, e.g., Shore Acres State Park, Cape Arago and the Oregon Dunes National Recreation Area.

Proximity to larger urban areas is fair. Eugene is 115 miles away. Roseburg, in the southern inland valley, is 77 miles away.

Summary: The Bay Area has a stable economic base. Tourism is a growing factor in providing stability. Proximity to the larger inland communities is reasonably good. Real estate is in good supply and is reasonable. The weather is slightly better than most of the coast. The population is large enough to support a business and the cultural amenities and health care facilities are very adequate. If a person is looking for a larger community on the Oregon coast, then the Bay Area is certainly worthy of consideration. Just remember that Highway 101 does not do justice to the area and one should explore the off highway areas.

Brookings (5,000 Pop.)

The Brookings area is known as the "Banana Belt" of Oregon. The climate is mild, with an average year around temperature of 53.5 degrees. During the winter months it is not unusual for Brookings to have some of the highest tempera-

Oregon

tures in Oregon. It is not unheard of for Brookings to have 80 degree temperatures in January.

Rain is a big thing in the area. Eighty inches of rain a year is not unusual but 80% of the precipitation comes in the winter during strong Pacific storms. The storms blow through and are often followed by several days of sun. The summers are mild and have relatively little rainfall.

Why is the weather different in Brookings than it is on the rest of coast? It has to do with atmospheric air pressure systems and protection from the northwestern weather by headlands to the north. Suffice it to say that the weather is pleasant a great deal of the time.

The economy is supported by fishing, tourism and forestry. A large food chain's headquarters is located in Brookings. With stores throughout the state, it is the sixth largest employer in Oregon. The cost of living is relatively low in the community. Brookings boasts of having the second lowest tax rate for a town its size in the state of Oregon.

Real estate opportunities are readily available. There are many beautiful home sites in the area and prices are reasonable by West coast standards. A newer three bedroom/two bath home can be found in the mid $150,000 range. Homes with ocean front will start in the low $300,000 and go up quickly. The Brookings market is tied to the health of the California real estate market. When homes are selling in California, the Brookings market benefits. It is a popular retirement community for many Californians.

The medical services reflect the small size of the community. Two hospitals are available, one at Crescent City and another at Gold Beach, both just 27 miles away. Ambulance and mercy flights are also available. There are nine doctors and eight dentist in the community.

The mild weather conditions have been largely responsible for drawing a large number of retirees. The weather allows gardening year around. In fact, Bookings is noted for the Easter lilies grown in the area. Ninety percent of the lilies sold in the United States and Canada come from the Brookings community.

The Chetco River affords fishermen the opportunity to go after the elusive steelhead and the magnificent salmon. This river, unlike most of the Oregon coast rivers, doesn't have the dangerous river bar. This fact gives Brookings one of the safest harbors on the coast. Consequently, sport fishing in the Pacific is readily available. Hunting is also good in the nearby mountains. Of course, hiking, beach combing, shellfish harvesting, whale watching, and kite flying are all available.

The cultural life of the community benefits from the large retirement population. With the advent of early retirements, this population is getting younger each year. The community has a performing arts center and has funded a band shell to start a summer concert series. A new library was recently completed.

Brookings might have one major drawback in that it is rather isolated from the larger urban areas. Portland is over 350 miles and Eugene is over 250 miles away from Brookings.

Summary: People want to move to Brookings; it is safe, comfortable, the cost of living is reasonable. There is lots to do, both indoors and out. Isolation might be a problem for some, but for others, the larger urban communities pale in comparison with the comfort and friendliness of this smaller community. As Eldon Gossett, a Realtor said, "Brookings is selling a way of life." If one wants natural beauty, a small community, gardening, and an active participation in the cultural life of the community, then this might be the place for such a person.

Willamette Valley

The Willamette Valley is about 150 miles long and 15 to 30 miles wide. The Coast Range borders it on the west and the Cascades separate it from Eastern Oregon. The Willamette and the McKenzie rivers are the main rivers in the valley.

It is a great agricultural region which is noted for fine wines, grass seed, Christmas trees, filberts and nursery stock. Forest products, high-tech manufacturing and shipping are also major players in the economy. The majority of the state's population is located in this region. Portland, the commercial, industrial and shipping center for Oregon, is located at the head the valley on the Willamette and Columbia rivers. Eugene, another major population center, is found 100 miles south of

Portland. A number of fine colleges and universities are located in the valley and some of the finest medical facilities in the Northwest are also found there.

The weather in the valley is mild. Winter temperatures can vary from the 50s to an occasional zero. The summer temperatures rarely get beyond the 90s. Rain is common place in the winters with occasional snows. Generally speaking, the weather is pleasant and not overly taxing.

Starting in the north and working south the following cities were visited: Silverton, Corvallis and Eugene.

Silverton (6,000 Pop.)

There is a saying in Silverton, "When one comes to Silverton, it is like coming home."

A small community, 42 miles south of Portland, it is an ideal retreat from the hustle and bustle of the larger urban area. Silverton is a peaceful place where the citizens know each other by first names and smiles go along with greetings. At the southern end of town one finds the start of some beautiful rolling hills carpeted with deep red soil, rich green fields and small stands of trees. Close to town, on the north, are neat farms and flourishing fields of flowers, berries, grapes, hops and Christmas trees. Much about Silverton is reminiscent of simpler days gone-by. It is clean and neat and shows the pride the citizens have in their community.

The economy centers on agriculture. In addition to the crops mentioned above, Silverton has the largest producing dairy in the state of Oregon. The community's economy is also supported by mobile and prefab home builders. A number of the Silverton residents commute to the larger urban areas of Salem and Portland for jobs and businesses and their incomes help stabilize Silverton's economy.

Real estate is, as one would expect, reasonable. A new three bedroom/two bath home can be found in the low $100,000s. A larger home with a view will cost in the high $100,000s and up. Small acreages with a home can be found in the high $100,000s. It should be noted that prices are heading up. The suburban areas in the north part of the Willamette Valley are becoming very popular.

The police department is a combination of paid staff backed by reservists. The fire department has some paid staff but relies mainly on volunteers. The crime rate is low and 911 is available.

The Silverton Hospital has 38 beds and is capable of delivering most of the services needed by a small community. Critical cases or cases needing highly specialized treatment are sent to the larger hospitals in nearby Salem or Portland. The hospital underwent substantial remodeling in the earlier part of the 90s.

The public schools provide a well rounded program. The elementary schools are broken into three age groups, K-3, 4-6, and 7-8. The high school focuses on grades 9-12. The high school not only provides a college prep program but also provides programs that deal with agriculture, technology and business.

College education is available in a number of nearby communities and on a extension basis in Silverton. Chemeketa Community College, located in Salem, provides a two year program. Willamette University, a prestigious private four year institution, is also located in Salem. Portland is home to Portland State University.

For air travel, Silverton residents rely on the Portland International Airport. The community maintains the Silverton Country Museum which give one a good idea of the bygone days of Silverton. Borland Gallery provides a home for the Silverton Art Association and features monthly exhibits of artists from around the country. Gallon House Bridge is the last covered bridge in Marion County. It got its name during the Prohibition era when it served as a drop-point for local bootleggers. As an additional point of interest, Oregon is home to over 50 covered bridges.

Cooley's Garden is the largest producer of bearded iris in the world and in May and June three million plants bloom in fields just west of Silverton.

What does Silverton do for fun and celebration? There is the Homer Davenport Days with a race down main street. What do they race? You guessed it - davenports or sometimes referred to as sofas. Of course, there is the Silverton Pet Parade which features pets, bikes, floats, bands, old car, young-

Oregon

sters and oldsters. Other celebrations include the Silverton Criterium Festival, involving bike racing; the Silverton Hills Strawberry Festival where the strawberry shortcake is beyond words, the Oregon Senior Olympics which has entrees from the entire West coast and finally, the wonderful Christmas Tree lighting ceremony.

Recreation in and around Silverton is not much different than in any rural community. The Silverton Reservoir provides for fishing, sailing and canoeing. There is fishing and hunting in the nearby streams and hills. The Cascade Mountains are close by where one can get away for fishing, hunting, hiking, camping, boating, climbing and on and on. Gardening is a favorite activity. The wonderful Oregon coast is about an hour away. Salem and Portland, with big town entertainment and shopping, are less than an hour away.

Summary: The rich soil of Silverton is a gardener's delight. The rolling hills with their red soil, green fields, and a dash of trees here and there, provide an artist a rich menu of scenes to capture on canvas or film. Silverton has a stable economy, the community services are very adequate. The community is safe and friendly and the citizens work hard to keep it that way. Indeed, when a person visits Silverton they do get the feeling that they have come home. Drop in on Silverton and see if you don't come away with the same feeling.

Corvallis (46,000 Pop.)

Corvallis is an attractive college town in the heart of the Willamette Valley. It is bounded on the west by the Coast Range and Mary's Peak, the highest point in the Range. To the east of town is the magnificent Willamette River, farm lands, foothills and finally the majestic Cascade Mountains.

Corvallis is a an orderly, clean and safe community. The age profile of the residents indicates that a majority of the people are less than 45 years old—a young community. The older parts of town have streets lined with giant deciduous trees and many neat older framed homes. The town is growing and there are a number of inviting developments springing up on the outskirts.

Oregon

Corvallis has attracted a number of high-tech firms which has significantly benefited the economy. Oregon State University is one of the drawing points for the high-tech industry. The University is the largest employer and the community benefits culturally and recreationally from O.S.U. In addition to the University and the high-tech industry, the economy is supported by agriculture, retail services, community medical services, wood products, food processing, and governmental agencies. This diversification makes for a very stable economy. Unemployment is low and the median family income is among the highest in the state.

Because of the desirability of the community, real estate is somewhat higher than in other Oregon communities. A new three bedroom/two bath home can be found in the mid $100,000. A small acreage plot with a home will start in the mid $100,000s and up. There are also a number of larger and more expensive homes in the Corvallis area. Nearby communities will have properties that are less expensive and within easy commuting distances.

Corvallis is a well run city and the community is actively involved in civic affairs. The police and fire departments are composed of paid staff. 911 is available. The public schools are excellent with approximately 75 % of the public school graduates going on to college. The test scores are some of the highest in the state and the students outperform the national norms. The community is financially supportive of the schools.

Comprehensive medical services are provided by the 188 bed Good Samaritan Hospital. The Corvallis Clinic is also available for medical services. If needed the larger hospitals of Eugene and Portland are relatively close.

Corvallis has an airport that is capable of handling private aircraft and charter flights. The Eugene airport, which is served by three airlines, and Portland International Airport provide commercial passenger service.

The benefits of having a major university in its midst are considerable when it comes to cultural impact. The University brings to the community many national speakers and entertainers, dramatic and musical productions, dance and two and three dimensional art programs. In addition to the cultural

Oregon

"bill of fare" offered by the University, Corvallis presents plays at the Majestic, Divincia Days in the park where science, technology and art are highlighted, and the Fall Festival which is an art only show. Linn-Benton Community College provides the community classes in the arts as well as other interesting pursuits.

The history of the region does not go unnoticed. There are a number of maintained historic sites, a historical museum, and three covered bridges to see and photograph.

Recreationally the community has a great deal to offer with the mountains, rivers and ocean being so close. Fishing on the Willamette River and the lesser streams is good, hunting in the mountains for the big game and in the lowlands for birds is rewarding, skiing opportunities are close by and hiking and camping are popular. The University, provides an exciting sports program and many instructional recreational activities.

Corvallis is about 70 miles from Portland and 40 miles from Eugene. The coast is about an hour away and the Cascades Mountains about the same.

Summary: Corvallis reminds one of a storybook college town. If one is interested in academic pursuits O.S.U. is among the finest in the Northwest. The economy is stable and unemployment is low. The housing is slightly higher than what has been found in other communities, but still reasonable compared with West coast prices. The public schools are first class. The city provides good services. Culturally and recreationally, there is plenty to do. Although the city is quite self sufficient, its proximity allows one to be in larger urban areas within a couple of hours. Corvallis has a great appeal as a place to settle down and enjoy many of the finer things life has to offer.

Eugene (120,000 Pop.)

Eugene, second largest community in Oregon, is located in the southern portion of the Willamette Valley. It is midway between the Cascades Mountains and the Pacific Ocean. Eugene is one of the most popular cities in Oregon. It is a community where people with very different lifestyles

Oregon

live together with great tolerance for each other. Two beautiful rivers pass through the city and it is bounded on the north and south by two buttes that are popular with hikers and nature lovers. The weather is generally comfortable. Winters are mild, snow is rare, rain is a frequent visitor in the winter. The summers are warm and humidity is not a problem.

Directly to the east of Eugene is the city of Springfield with a population of 45,000. Highway Interstate 5 separates the two cities. Except for different municipal governments, the cities can be viewed as a whole.

The economy is supported by firms dealing with wood products, high-tech manufacturing, agriculture and food processing, recreational vehicle fabrication, the University of Oregon, and regional medical and governmental services. This broad diversity makes for a very stable economy. Recently, several large high-tech firms have located in Eugene, making for an even stronger economy. The cost of living is slightly higher than the national average.

Real estate prices have recovered from the lows experienced in the 1980s. The trend in the mid 90s has been upward. Even with this trend, the prices are still considered to be reasonable when compared to many metropolitan areas in the West. A new three bedroom/two bath home can be found in the in the mid $100,000s. View property is available in the upper $100,000s and higher. There are a number of smaller communities within commuting distance that will have less expensive prices. If one is interested in a home with small acreage, it can be found at a reasonable price.

There are two hospitals in the area. Sacred Heart General Hospital is a regional medical center that provides a comprehensive medical program. The smaller McKenzie-Willamette Hospital is located in Springfield. A highly acclaimed sports medicine program is available in Eugene and a number of world class athletes have been treated there.

The Eugene public school district is recognized statewide as outstanding. It provides a comprehensive educational program for over 18,000 pupils. There are many alternative programs offered by the school district. Two programs that perhaps are harbingers of the future, are the language immer-

Oregon

sion schools that are available in Japanese, Spanish and French languages and the International School.

The University of Oregon with its 18,000 students has a great impact on the community. It is located in the southeastern portion of the city on a beautiful campus. The University, besides being a wonderful place for learning, enhances the cultural and entertainment environment of the Eugene area.

Lane Community College is an institution that is oriented to serving the community of Eugene and a number of other communities in the region. It serves over 35,000 students a year. Besides its Associates Degree programs, it provides the community with many interesting and valuable continuing education classes.

In addition to the two fine institutions mentioned above, there is the Northwest Christian College. It is a liberal arts college whose academic program is guided by Christian beliefs. Undergraduate majors are offered in business administration, speech communications, psychology, intercultural studies, pre-law, music, and ministry.

Eugene has a full service airport that provides commercial passenger and freight service. Service is provided by Horizon Air, United Airlines and United Express. Flights serve the West coast and connect with national and international flights.

Eugene is a place where it is possible to enjoy the finer things of life in a relaxed and warm atmosphere. The Hult Center for the Performing Arts, which has received national acclaim, is the focal point for much of the city's cultural and entertainment activity. The Center hosts top name national and international performers in music, dance and drama. Locally, Eugene can boast of having ballet, a symphony, opera, dramatic and musical productions.

The University provides a variety of events which add to the rich cultural environment of the community. National and international speakers are brought to the community by the University. Of course, the schools of drama and music do their part to provide high caliber performances. The Oregon Bach Festival is sponsored by the Music School and theater productions are presented in the University's Robinson Theater.

Oregon

There are a number of modern libraries in the community, plus seven museums and a number of art galleries. When it comes to festivals and celebration, one only has to start with the Lane County Fair to get a good idea of the wholesome values of this community. There is also Art in the Vineyard, the Asian Celebration, the Eugene Celebration, plus any number of crafts fairs.

Eugene is in an outstanding location for recreation. The McKenzie and the Willamette rivers are tops for sport fishing, canoeing and kayaking. The mountains are within an hour and there are countless lakes and streams which also provide championship fishing opportunities. Boating, hiking, camping, rock climbing, hunting, downhill skiing, cross country skiing, and snowmobiling are all popular. The ocean and it's recreational opportunities are also within an hour.

Eugene is known throughout the nation as the "Track Capital of the World." The University's football and basketball teams are outstanding and community support of the programs is almost fanatical. The region has eight golf courses, more than 50 tennis courts, a number of swimming pools, many miles of jogging and bike paths and canoeing is available on the rivers and nearby lakes. Sailing is popular on the Fern Ridge Reservoir.

Eugene is ideally located to take advantage of all Oregon has to offer. The drier eastern Oregon is within two hours, the large urban city of Portland is a couple hours away, the mountains and the coast are relatively close. What more could a person want?

Summary: Eugene is indeed a place that people like and are not anxious to leave. Many a University student, upon graduation, will take a lower paying job if they can just to remain in Eugene. The city has excellent services, the hospitals can handle any illness, the schools are first rate, the economy is stable and cultural, entertainment and recreational opportunities abound. Housing is a bit high but compared to much of the West coast it is very reasonable. All in all, Eugene is a real hit with the folks who live there and it might be just the kind of place you have been looking for.

Umpqua and Rogue Valleys

Upon leaving the Willamette Valley and venturing south, one is soon confronted by a series of valleys that coexist with beautiful rivers, vast forests and rugged mountains. Such an environment promotes industries that will capitalize on a region's natural resources.

Wood products, agriculture and tourism are the main economic drivers for these valleys. The forests start to change from the Douglas fir trees, so prominent in the Willamette Valley, to forest where pine and oak take over.

The valleys have relatively mild winters. Most of the snow falls on the high hills that surround the valley communities. The summers can be very hot with temperatures above 100 degrees. The falls and springs are normally quite delightful.

Roseburg (19,000 Pop.)

Roseburg is located about 70 miles south of Eugene. It is in a valley which is nestled among some heavily forested hills. The larger area in which Roseburg is located is often referred to as "The Hundred Valleys of the Umpqua," the Umpqua being the main river of the area.

Roseburg is not a new town. To the visitor it might seem that one has stepped back in time. The central part of town, the historic downtown, is much as one would imagine it was in the "fifties"—a time when life was simpler and the pace slower. So as not to be misunderstood, Roseburg also has its more contemporary aspects, i. e., shopping malls and new housing developments. Newer business areas are growing along Interstate 5. Residential areas are scattered throughout the city with the newer section in the northwest part of the city. Roseburg is popular with retirees.

The economy of the area is stable. It relies on governmental agencies, wood products, manufacturing, agriculture and tourism for its strong base. The "spotted owl" restrictions have had some limiting impact on the wood product industry but industrial diversification in the valley has helped soften any losses.

Oregon

Real estate prices are about average for a Northwest non-urban town like Roseburg. A new three bedroom/two bath house will run in the low $100,000s and up. Older homes with some acreage can be found in the higher $100,000s. There are a number of homes on small acreage and ranches available for purchase. River frontage is also available on the north and south Umpqua River.

Police and fire protection is provided by paid staff. This community has a low crime rate. 911 services are available. The community does not have a public bus system which is perhaps a drawback for some people. The Veterans Administration Medical Center (417 beds), the Douglas County Hospital (123 beds) and the Mercy Medical Hospital (111 beds) are all located in Roseburg.

The public schools are large enough to provide a well rounded educational program. The enrollment is close to 7,000 pupils. A high percentage, approximately 79%, of the graduates go on to higher education. Higher educational opportunities are provided by Umpqua Community College, located five miles north of Roseburg. Extension courses are available through the Oregon universities located in Eugene and Corvallis.

Commercial air passenger service is available in Eugene, to the north, or Medford, to the south. A smaller airport, which services private and charter aircraft, is available in Roseburg.

The Umpqua Actors Community Theatre and the local community college provide an active theater and musical environment for the community. The musical "menu" is added to by the Roseburg Community Concert Association, the Umpqua Symphony Association, Music in the Half Shell programs, The Vintage Singers, a chamber orchestra and a community band.

There are a number of festivals which include: the Blue Grass Festival, the Art and Jazz Festival, the Wine Festival and Graffiti Week - a return to the "fifties." Perhaps unique to Roseburg is the Umpqua Fishery Enhancement Derby, a catch and release affair, established to raise money for habitat restoration and stream enhancement. Another unique event is the Douglas County Lamb and Wool Show.

Oregon

Roseburg is the home of the Douglas County Museum and the new Douglas County Library. The Umpqua Valley Arts Center features regular art exhibits throughout the year. Also, one will find a number of fine art galleries and antique facilities enlivening the cultural environment of the city. If one likes to volunteer, there are numerous opportunities available in Roseburg.

Recreational opportunities are almost to numerous to mention. This area is located with two very beautiful and bountiful rivers in close proximity. In addition, the Cascade and Coast Range mountains are close by. The Oregon coast is less than two hours away. Roseburg's proximity to the rivers, mountains and beaches open up all the outdoor recreational possibilities for which one could wish. The city maintains a rich program of recreational and entertainment opportunities. With a growing season of 217 days, gardening is very popular.

Roseburg is less than two hours away from Eugene or Medford. Portland is 177 miles to the north.

Summary: The Roseburg community has a stable economy, the city services are good, as are the medical and educational services. Cultural opportunities are plentiful. Recreational opportunities are one of the area's highlights. The winter weather is mild and the summers are dry and warm. This area's climate has often been compared with Italy and southern France. This is an area that is popular with retirees. If one is looking for a stable community that focuses on the family and providing a safe and wholesome environment, then Roseburg is worth a look.

Grants Pass (18,800 Pop.)

High above the main street of Grants Pass hangs a sign that says "It's the Climate." The sign is certainly right about one thing, the climate does make Grants Pass a great place but it does not tell the whole story. As Paul Harvey says, "And now for the rest of the story." Grants Pass is a small, friendly community. People are drawn to this community because of its healthy environment, its scenic beauty, its cultural and rec-

Oregon

reational opportunities and the reputation of the wild and untamed Rogue River.

Grants Pass is surrounded by high hills and mountains, with green forests of evergreens and beautiful oaks. On any given day from a high view point, one sees forest covered hills, one after another disappearing in the mist and haze of the majestic mountains. This is also a city where the downtown has buildings that appear on the National Historic Register while at the same time new developments are springing up on the outskirts.

The economy of the community is supported by wood products, agriculture, tourism and some new high-tech industry. The wood products industries are not as strong as they were and diversification has taken up some of the slack created by their downturn. The local community college has been instrumental in assisting the community in retraining some of the local work force which has helped to support the local economy.

A new three bedroom/two bath home can be purchased in the low to mid $100,000 range. View and river frontage homes will start in the mid $100,000 and go up quickly. Homes on small acreages start in the mid $100,000. There appears to be numerous opportunities in the small acreage category. There are even a number of properties that fit the ranch category for sale in the Grants Pass area.

Grants Pass is a large enough community that it can provide good services to its residents. The police force is a paid staff. Of the seven fire departments, two are private. 911 services are available.

There are two hospitals in the community. The Josephine Memorial Hospital is a 81 bed facility. Southern Oregon Medical Center is a 63 bed facility. Both of these facilities provide services for the majority of the medical needs of the community. Since both hospitals are relatively small they can secure support for highly specialized treatments from the larger hospitals in Medford and Eugene.

There are two school districts that serve Grants Pass. The county district enrolls 6,000 pupils and serves the majority of residents outside the city limits. District 7 serves students that live within the city limits of Grants Pass. District 7 has an enrollment of approximately 4,000 pupils. Both districts are large enough to provide comprehensive educational programs. As with the vast majority of Oregon's school districts, Grants Pass and the county district provide excellent educational programs.

Rogue Community College plays an important educational role in the community. It serves close to 10,000 people each year. The college provides a vocational and technical program, a lower division college transfer program, and a community adult education program.

Commercial air service for passengers and freight is available at the airports in Medford and Eugene. Grants Pass has the Josephine County Airport which has a 4,000 foot runway. It provides fuel and maintenance services.

Grants Pass offers some first class cultural and entertainment opportunities. The Rogue Music Theatre puts on productions that are spectacular. Where in the "big city" can one go to a production of the "King and I" for $12.00? These are very professional productions and are treasured by the community. The summer productions are performed under the stars at the Rogue Community College's amphitheater. Fall and winter productions are performed indoors at the Rogue Building on the Community College's campus.

In addition to the Music Theatre group, there is the Barnstormers Little Theatre group. The performers are locals who have talents and lots of energy. The Barnstormers have been presenting a wide variety of plays for a number of years. It has the distinct honor of being the oldest community theatre in the state.

The Rogue Valley Symphony performs in Grants Pass. It usually presents three concerts dealing with the classics. The Symphony also performs in nearby Medford and Ashland. The concerts are sponsored by the Rogue Valley Symphony Association and Southern Oregon State College. The nearness of the communities of Medford, Jacksonville and Ashland, makes a number of other cultural and entertainment events available to the citizens of Grants Pass. Some other attractions are the pari-mutuel horse racing that takes place during June, the Grower's Market on Saturdays from April to November, a number of art galleries, and the museum.

Oregon

When it comes to recreation the river draws most of the attention. The Rogue is famous for its white waters. Zane Grey spent time in the remote stretches of the Rogue. There are a number of fine fishing rivers in the vicinity of Grants Pass. In addition to the Rogue there are the Illinois, the Applegate, the Chetco and Smith rivers. These rivers provide salmon and steelhead as well as some trout.

The Rogue Valley and the surrounding mountains offer hiking, camping, float trips, kayaking, gold panning and thrilling jet boat rides. Downhill skiing is available at Mt. Ashland, just 60 miles to the south.

The city is well aware of the need for recreational opportunities for it residents. The newer All Sports Park is an example of the city's commitment. The Park provides four Little League fields, an American Legion and Babe Ruth baseball field each, a soccer field, and tennis, basketball, volleyball, racquetball and handball courts. In addition the Park has jogging trails, playgrounds, picnic areas and shelters.

Grants Pass is located about 140 miles south of Eugene and 245 miles south of Portland. The communities of Medford and Ashland are less than 40 miles from Grants Pass. Medford, Ashland and Grants Pass form a "mega" community when it comes to shopping, recreation and entertainment.

Summary: Grants Pass is a delightful place with great beauty, a pleasant climate, and a rich cultural and recreational environment. The Rogue River, with its scenic beauty, is spectacular. This is a city that is popular with retirees. The proximity, to larger communities is good, and health, civic and educational services are readily available. There is a wholesome atmosphere surrounding Grants Pass and it should be one of the communities that receive further investigation.

Medford (53,000 Pop.)

This is the largest city in southwestern Oregon. It is located in the southern end of the Rogue Valley. Medford is the commercial and medical center of the region. The city is a mixture of the old and new. It is located in a broad valley with surrounding hills of golden grasses, accented with the rich browns of the soil and rock, and the greens of the mighty oaks. The valley has a rugged yet delicate appeal.

The economic base is dependent on wood products, medical services, agriculture and food processing, governmental agencies and tourism. This diversification leads to a very stable economy.

Real estate prices are reasonable. A new three bedroom/two bath home can be purchased in the low $100,000s. View homes will start in the mid $100,000s. Small acreage plots with homes are available in and around Medford. There are many beautifully built homes in the Medford area and their cost will range from the high $100,000s up to the mid $200,000s. Hot summers make private swimming pools more common than one normally finds in the rest of the Northwest.

The services of the city are on par with any city of equivalent size. The police and fire departments have paid staff. 911 service is available. The city bus service also serves Ashland which is 12 miles to the south. The Medford airport has commercial passenger service on three airlines.

There is strong school support. The public school enrollment is about 11,000 students. This allows the school district to support a strong educational program. Something unique to Medford is the Medford Educational Institute which is a national nonprofit education information center. There are two institutions of higher learning located in nearby communities. Thirty miles to the north in Grants Pass is Rogue Community College. Southern Oregon State College (SOC) is located close by in Ashland and is a 4-year degree granting institution.

There are three hospital facilities in Medford. The 305 bed Rogue Valley Medical Center is a large full-service medical center. Providence Hospital and Medical Center is somewhat smaller but still capable of providing most of the services needed by a given population. The Medford Clinic is a professional corporation owned by 63 doctors. It provides services normally associated with a modern medical clinic.

Culturally, Medford doesn't take a back seat to any city its size. Medford is only 12 miles from Ashland and its famous Oregon Shakespeare Festival In addition to this thespian effort, Medford has a number of active community theater groups.

Musically, the nearby community of Jacksonville produces the Peter Britt Music Festival This festival spotlights world class performers who bring classical, jazz, country and folk music to the audiences. Other opportunities for entertainment are provided by the Medford Civic Ballet, the Oregon Cabaret Theater, the Rogue Opera Association, the Rogue Valley Symphony and the State Ballet of Oregon.

The proximity of the mountains and wild exciting rivers make hiking, hunting, fishing, boating, whitewater rafting, camping, and biking, very popular recreational activities. Crater Lake and beautiful Diamond Lake are close by and add to the fascination of this region for hiking and camping. Winter activities include skiing at Mt. Ashland as well as snowmobiling and cross country skiing. A person can get to the ocean with all its recreational opportunities in less than two hours. One will also find nearby bike and nature trails, tennis courts, 5 golf courses, swimming clubs and countless other possible diversions.

Medford, as a community, is quite self-sufficient. If one wants to visit larger urban areas, Eugene is 166 miles to the north and Portland is 273 miles up Interstate 5. San Francisco is 373 miles to the south. For those who might like to gamble a bit, Reno is 304 miles to the southeast, a 6 to 7 hour drive.

Summary: Medford offers a healthy and vigorous lifestyle. It has good civic services and the medical facilities are capable of handling the needs of its population. Real estate prices are reasonable and there is an adequate supply of homes. Cultural and recreational opportunities abound. The cost of living is reasonable. The climate is mild and snow is not a great problem. The summers are warm, and sometimes, just plain hot, but humidity is low. Medford has a lot going for it.

Oregon

Ashland (18,000 Pop.)

Ashland, is an amazing community. It has the charm of a small picturesque town and yet its cultural, entertainment, and recreational opportunities can match or exceed any number of large urban communities. One only has to drive down the main street to be impressed with the attractiveness of the community. The forested hills and mountains to the west and the rich farm lands and beautiful oaks to the east provide a unique backdrop to the town and its world famous Oregon Shakespeare Festival which operates eight months a year, February through October. This organization is responsible for producing a number of beautifully staged Shakespearian and contemporary plays during its season. What isn't well known is that the Festival also includes other classic and contemporary plays in its repertoire.

The economy of the community is dependent upon tourism, wood products and education. The big draw for tourism is the Oregon Shakespeare Festival, the wonderful climate of the area and the recreational opportunities. The reliance upon timber and wood product is expected to decline in the future, a consequence of governmental regulations. Education's main contributor to the economy is Southern Oregon State College. It should be added that the U.S. Fish and Wildlife Forensic Lab is located in Ashland—evidence of the community's efforts to diversify.

Due to Ashland's popularity, real estate prices are higher than the surrounding communities. New three bedroom/two bath homes will cost in the mid $100,000s and up. View homes, and there are numerous view sites, will start in the low $200,000 and go up quickly. Nice homes on small acreages will start in the low $200,000s. It should be pointed out that this desirable community has one of the lower property taxes in the state.

The police and fire personnel are paid professionals. The community has 911 services. The 58 bed Ashland Community Hospital provides medical services for most of the needs of the community. A short distant away, in Medford, is Rogue Valley Medical Center which is capable of augmenting Ashland's medical services.

Oregon

Ashland's public schools enroll approximately 3,500 students. The school district is well supported by the community and is capable of providing a comprehensive educational program. Approximately 50% of the graduating class goes on to higher education. The community has not failed to pass a general budget or bond levy for over 20 years.

Southern Oregon State College (SOC) is located in Ashland and enriches the community's educational and cultural opportunities. It is a multi-program institution with an enrollment of about 4,300 students. The College provides extension classes for another 3,500 students. With the college so close, the public schools can provide college early entrance classes for high school students.

Commercial passenger and freight air transportation is available at the Rogue Valley International Airport at Medford, just 20 miles north of Ashland. Ashland has a small full service airport for private aircraft.

Not only does Ashland have the Oregon Shakespeare Festival, but it also has nine other theatre groups which provide musicals, comedies and experimental theatre. These programs go on all year.

All of the theatrical programs are highly dependent on volunteers. The community readily responds to this need. In addition to Ashland's dramatic productions, there is also ample opportunity to enjoy musical productions. Folk singing, opera and chamber music are common occurrences in the community. The College and several other organizations in the county add to the musical menu of Ashland.

There are a large number of art galleries in the community. The galleries annually promote the "Taste of Ashland" which includes wine tasting, good food and great art.

The College and the Jackson County Library System provide the community with modern library facilities. Recreational opportunities present one with a vast number of enjoyable activities. Mt. Ashland and Mt. Shasta are close by with downhill and cross country skiing. Snowmobiling and ice fishing are also available in the mountains.

There are two exciting rivers that can provide first class fishing and memorable whitewater rafting experiences. The Cascade Mountains with trails and gorgeous lakes make hik-

Oregon

ing, camping, fishing and hunting within easy reach. Crater Lake, the deepest lake in the U.S., is near by. If people want to enjoy the Pacific Ocean, then a three to four hour ride will deliver them to the beach.

Ashland has one of the most attractive city parks to be seen anyplace in the Northwest. Lithia Park was born when, in 1908, the women of Ashland wanted to bring some beauty to the town. It is a gem and no one should miss enjoying its beauty and tranquility.

Golf is becoming a major sport in the Ashland and Medford area. Presently, there are five golf courses in the immediate area with seven more on the drawing board. There is some talk of developing destination resorts in the area.

Ashland is located 15 miles from the California border. This community is popular with folks retiring and relocating from California. People from Oregon and Washington who are tired of the wetter climate in the north are drawn to Ashland for its dryer climate and rich cultural and recreational environment.

San Francisco is 365 miles to the south and Portland is 290 miles to the north. Between Medford and Ashland all the services one could want are readily available, consequently the distances from large urban areas is not necessarily a drawback.

Summary: Ashland is fantastic. It is small but not too small. It has a rich cultural and recreational environment. People like to be involved with what goes on in the community. The crime rate is low. The economy is stable. Property taxes are relatively low. The schools are good. Medical services are superior. An excellent college is located in Ashland. Real estate prices are somewhat high but this can be overcome by locating a short distant from Ashland. Ashland is indeed a very desirable place to live.

Central Oregon

Central Oregon, for the purpose of this discussion, is defined as the area that lies on the eastern slopes of the Cascade Mountains and extending approximately 75 miles to the

Oregon

east. This region run from the Columbia River, on the north, to the Oregon/California border, on the south. Most of the region is considered high desert, with altitudes ranging from 2,000 to over 4,000 feet. The very northern portion fronts the Columbia River and consequently is within 100 feet of sea level. The rest of the eastern portion of the state will be considered Eastern Oregon.

Central Oregon is a very large area. The majority of the population is along the Highway 97 corridor and in communities fronting the Columbia River. Five communities were visited. They were Klamath Falls on the south, Bend, Redmond and Sisters in the center and Hood River on the Columbia.

The eastern portions of the region can best be described as having an abundance of sagebrush, juniper, basalt outcropping, sand, rattlesnakes, coyotes, and cattle. There are a number of large cattle and hay ranches. The northern portion of Central Oregon is fairly dry but lends itself to great fields of golden grains and as one nears the Columbia River, orchards. In the western sections, on the eastern slopes of the Cascades, one finds large ponderosa pine forests, lakes, rivers and stream, beautiful meadows and the awe inspiring snowcapped peaks of the Cascade Mountains. This is the territory of the huge Upper Klamath Lake, jewel-like Crater Lake, the snow covered peaks of the Cascades.

Central Oregon is one of the fastest growing regions in Oregon. This is especially true in the Bend, Redmond and Sisters area. Even though it is growing rapidly there is still plenty of room.

The major industries in the region consist of agriculture, wood products, and tourism. The climate is such that the summers are warm and sunny, with cool nights. The highs will get into the 90s and 100s. Spring and fall are usually a delight. The winters are cold, but not severely so, and most of the precipitations comes in the form of snow and a small amount of rain. The closer one is to the mountains the more snow and rain one will experience. The region's winter temperatures will get into the low teens and on rare occasions colder. Winter ice storms are experienced along the Columbia.

Oregon

The annual precipitation averages 30 inches along the Columbia and 12-14 inches for the greater portions of the region south of the river. The dryness of the climate in the majority of the region makes for a comfortable environment. Many folks from the west side of the mountains come to the east side for the sun. This is true not only in the summer but also in the winter.

Highway 97 runs the full length of the Central Oregon corridor. It is two lanes most of the way. It carries a great deal of truck traffic, since this is the route many truckers chose when coming from the south and serving the eastern parts of the Northwest. The road is well maintained and easy to drive. The highway causes some congestion in the towns of Bend and Redmond.

Seven highways wind their way across the Cascade Mountains which make the Willamette Valley and southern valleys easily accessible. The city of Hood River, in the north, is on Interstate 84. This is a fine four lane highway and doesn't cause noticeable congestion for the bulk of the cities along its route.

The Columbia River Gorge National Scenic Area is located in the northern portion of Central Oregon. It is absolutely beautiful with the great river, steep cliffs, gorgeous orchards and majestic Mt. Hood and Mt. Adams bordering the north and south sides of the Columbia Gorge. There are two scenic waterways, the Deschutes and John Day. They both flow into the Columbia River and provide not only some beautiful and rugged scenery but some excellent fishing and whitewater rafting opportunities.

Central Oregon is a recreational treasure. Skiing is big in this region, with mountains like Bachelor and Hood providing magnificent slopes. Of course, there is snowmobiling, cross country skiing, snowshoeing, camping, fishing, hunting, backpacking, golf, mountain climbing, rock climbing, bird watching, windsurfing, boating, water skiing, tennis, biking and just about anything else a person can think of along the lines of outdoor recreation.

The cost of living in these areas is close to the national average. It is less in some of the smaller communities. Klamath Falls and Redmond have very reasonable real estate prices. Bend, Sisters and Hood River have the highest real estate prices in the region, but even these are reasonable when compared with the larger urban areas in Western Oregon.

Central Oregon is for the person who likes to have a lot of outdoor recreation and who enjoys four seasons. In the larger communities the services are very adequate and numerous cultural opportunities are available. Central Oregon has become very popular and it is not hard to see why.

Hood River (17,000 Pop.)

Hood River is a port city on the mighty Columbia River. It is located in the Columbia Gorge and the downtown is perched on a hillside over looking the river. Hood River is most noted for its fruit orchards and strong winds which delight the windsurfers. It is located close to Mount Hood which makes it a convenient base for skiing and hiking trips to the mountain.

Hood River scenery is grand from every aspect. Snow-capped Mt. Hood and Mt. Adams are visible from the town, as is the river and the green hills, beyond. Besides the breathtaking beauty of the region, one also finds this area to be recreational wonderland. The great river and the close by mountains act as magnets drawing tourist from all over the world.

The downtown is like many hillside towns found on large rivers in the Midwest and East. It has brick business building and large older view homes on tree shaded streets. Stern-wheelers and tourist boats make Hood River a port of call as do the barges that take away the agricultural crops of the area.

The economy is supported primarily by fruit growing and processing and the nearby forests. Tourism has become a boon to the Hood River area in recent years, especially with the growth of windsurfing on the river. With this growth has come a sizable cottage industry. The business community is working hard to promote Hood River as a base for tourists who are considering the winter sports offered by the Mt. Hood area. Mt. Hood Meadows, a popular ski area, is only thirty-five miles to the south.

Oregon

Land in Hood River county is not as available for housing as one might expect. The Federal government controls about 63 percent of the land. The remaining 37 percent is privately owned with 5 % designated for residential development and the other 32 % being taken up with farms and private forests. These factor, in addition to Hood River's attractiveness and proximity to Portland, precipitate higher than expected real estate prices.

A three bedroom/two bath home can be found in the mid $100,000 price range. View homes will be more expensive and the view lots are quite high. There are some stately homes overlooking the river, that if refurbished would be classics. Costs are lower on the north side of the river and availability is better. The north side of the river is readily accessible over the Singing Bridge which goes from Hood River to Bingen, Washington.

Fire protection is provided by a combination of paid full-time and volunteer personnel. The police protection, depending on location, is a combination of city police and county sheriff personnel. Crime is relatively low and there is no tolerance for gangs in Hood River.

Hood River has a newly renovated hospital capable of handling most problems. Those cases of a more critical nature, such as heart surgery, have Portland hospitals available.

The schools in Hood River, like most of Oregon schools, are good. The teacher/pupil ratio is good and the district is large enough to have a fairly broad curriculum. Post high school education is available at Columbia Gorge Community College, 21 miles upriver, at The Dalles. Portland and its surrounding communities have a number of two and four year institutions also available.

Hood River has an airport that provides for general aviation. For commercial service one must go the Portland International Airport, 55 miles to the west.

The community has amateur theater, and local music groups. There are galleries with works by local artists. One of the advantages of living in Hood River is that a person is about one hour away from Portland and its cultural and entertainment opportunities.

Recreation around Hood River is similar to what it is for the Central Oregon region i.e. hiking, fishing, hunting, skiing, etc. The activities that are unique to Hood River and the Gorge are windsurfing and paragliding. The strong winds are beneficial to both activities. Hood River is noted worldwide as one of the premier windsurfing areas.

The proximity to Portland is a real strong point for Hood River. It means one can live in a more relaxed community and still enjoy the excitement of the big city.

Summary: Hood River is a very attractive community. It is in the Columbia River Gorge National Scenic Area. The orchards in the spring and summer are gorgeous with their blossoms and green rows of beautiful trees. The Gorge with its blue river, brightly colored windsurfing sails and dark brown cliffs is right out of the *National Geographic* magazines we all devoured in our youth. The perfect version of what a snow-capped mountain should look like will be found in the images presented by Mt. Hood and Mt. Adams. The town is clean, neat, safe and large enough to provide adequate services. The availability of residential property is somewhat limiting. Hood River presents an atmosphere that is relaxed and full of beauty. It is a must for someone who want lots of beauty, enjoys outdoor recreation and is not yet quite ready to leave the big city completely behind.

Redmond (10,000 Pop.)

Redmond is part of the Central Oregon triangle composed of the towns of Bend, Redmond and Sisters. Each town is unique while at the same time enjoying the natural and recreational benefits common to all Central Oregon. Redmond offers a community that is peaceful and calm.

The economy of Redmond profits from the tourist traffic, agriculture, light industry and aviation. As with Bend, Redmond also suffers from the traffic associated with Highway 97. They have been able to soften the traffic impact on its downtown by instituting one-way traffic.

The streets in the older part of town are tree lined and sprinkled with some fine older homes. Residential housing developments are springing up on the outskirts of the town. These newer developments are providing housing alternatives for both Redmond and nearby Bend.

Real estate in the Redmond area is probably the most reasonable of the surrounding communities. Three bedroom/two bath home prices will start in the $90,000s and go up. View property can be purchased for $140,000 and up. Small ranchettes can also be found in a reasonable price range.

Redmond has a low crime rate. The city provides its own police services, while the outlying areas are served by the Deschutes County Sheriff and the state police. Fire protection is provided by a combination of city and county firefighters. The fire service has personnel trained in emergency medicine. The ambulance service is provided by the fire department. Somewhat unique to Redmond is the practice where a citizen can pay $45 a year for ambulance service, should they ever need it.

Redmond has a small hospital that is capable of handling most of the problems a person would have. Cases that require more comprehensive treatment are forwarded to St. Charles Medical Center in Bend or to a Portland hospital.

The schools in Redmond are like most of the schools in Oregon, very good. The district serves approximately 4,700 youths and this make the district large enough to provide a well balanced curriculum. Higher educational needs are satisfied by Central Oregon Community College located in Bend. Extension courses are also available from some of Oregon's four-year institutions.

The airport is a gem in the crown of Redmond. It is a modern complex with a 7,000 foot hard surfaced runway, an attractive terminal and services for both commercial and private aircraft. The airport is served by Horizon and United Express.

Redmond is not a large town but has all the basic services covered. The town is growing by 4 to 5 % annually. It is benefiting from the growth in Bend and provides a less expensive living alternative.

Redmond and Bend share cultural opportunities, with the larger Bend providing a broader spectrum of activities. As for recreation, Redmond offers the same outdoor opportuni-

Oregon

ties that exist in Central Oregon. One outstanding recreational opportunity located close by Redmond is the beautiful Eagle Crest Resort with its two, soon to be three, 18 hole golf courses. Also common to this region is rock climbing at Smith Rock State Park and skiing at Mt. Bachelor.

Portland is 144 miles to the northwest and Eugene is 126 miles to the west. Both these urban areas are assessable by good roads. Crossing the mountains in the winter can be a bit troublesome.

Summary: Redmond is a good alternative to escaping the higher prices of Bend. It is located close to recreational and cultural opportunities. This is a town that will grow and could possibility be a good small business location. Redmond lacks the "pizzazz" of Bend but it is a wholesome town with a little slower pace. The schools and community services are good. Good medical services are convenient. Housing is available and more is being built. There are some nice, older homes that will shine with some paint and patching. All in all, if one likes the Central Oregon area and needs to be frugal, then Redmond has great possibilities.

Sisters (820 Pop.)

Sisters is a small community west of Bend and Redmond. It is part of the beautiful Central Oregon triangle. Sisters is close to the mountains and this is where the beautiful and stately ponderosa pine trees take over from the juniper and sage brush found in the dryer portions of the region.

The community has some of the most splendid mountain views of anywhere in the United States. The majestic Three Sisters with their snow crowned peaks, the cinnamon barked ponderous pines, along with the green/gold meadows, and the pinks of a summer sunset present a western scene that is beyond description. (It is at a time like this if one looks closely at the distant hazy horizon one would swear he could see the spirit of the "Duke" watching over the valley and its people.)

The tourist industry and agriculture provide the basis of the economy. Tourists are fascinated by the busy main street whose buildings present an "old western" theme. The main

Oregon

street is always busy with tourist stopping for some shopping and a bite to eat.

A newer three bedroom/two bath home will start in the neighborhood of $130,000 and up. Real estate prices, on the average, are higher than one will find in Bend and Redmond. The upscale Black Butte Resort area has homes that will fall in a range of $300,000 to $900,000. Real estate prices reflect the desirability of the Sisters area.

The police services are provided by the city staff and the county sheriff. Fire protection is primarily provided by volunteers, with a small paid support staff. 911 is coordinated by the county. Ambulance service is available. The Black Butte Resort has its own police and fire service. There are two medical clinics in Sisters. Patients needing hospital care are sent to either the small Redmond hospital or to St. Charles Medical Center in Bend. The school system is small but ranks high in the state of Oregon relative to achievement. The enrollment is about 1,000 pupils.

When it comes to cultural opportunities the citizens of Sisters can easily access the events of Redmond and Bend. Bend, being the largest community, provides the bulk of the opportunities. Sisters does have a number of community events that provide for involvement of folks. For example, there is the Sisters Art Stroll, the Sisters Rodeo, the Quilt Show, the High Mountains Dixieland Jazz Festival and the Saturday Market.

Recreational opportunities are abundant. The mountains, lakes, stream, forest, and ranches provide for about every outdoor recreational opportunity Central Oregon has to offer. If one wants a close up view of the perky llama or the mighty elk, there are ranches that raise the creatures. There is nothing better than watching llamas romping with each other under the sunlit skies of Central Oregon.

Sisters is located on the major highway that take one across the Cascade Mountains to the Willamette Valley. Portland is 160 miles to the northwest and Eugene is 110 miles to the west.

Summary: Sisters is small but it is close to larger communities where additional shopping, medical services and cultural

Oregon

opportunities exist. It is about as close as one can come to a "Western town". It is a peaceful community with lots of outdoor recreational opportunities. The real estate prices are higher than some of the other areas in Central Oregon but the community is a very desirable place to live. Tourist traffic flows through town on the main street almost year around. This is because in the summers people come for the high desert heat, camping, fishing and golf, etc. In the winter, most of the cars passing through town have ski racks. Indeed, skiing at nearby Mt. Bachelor is a "downhillers" dream. If a person is looking for a western theme, peace, friendly folks, and great outdoor recreational opportunities, Sisters fits the bill.

Bend (29,000 Pop.)

There is something about Bend that seems to draw people to it. Perhaps it's the town's vitality. As one drives through the town they can not help but be impressed with the commercial activity. Then again, Bend might be found attractive because of its pleasant residential areas, the vast park system with its beautiful downtown park, or the college, or the wonderful climate, or the abundant recreational opportunities, or perhaps, it is the cultural activity of the community. What ever it is, the area is attractive and Bend has been discovered.

The economy of Bend depends on the tourist trade, wood products and the services it provides to the Central Oregon region. The cost of living in Bend is slightly higher than the national average and considerably lower than some of the larger urban areas of the West. The population is growing everyday. The Bend area is especially popular with retired folks. From 1990 to 1994 the overall population grew 43.75 percent. In Deschutes County, where Bend is located, the growth during the same period was 19.4 percent, while the state of Oregon grew 8 percent.

Bend provides any number of attractive housing developments for the newcomers. The are a number of beautiful golf courses with residences surrounding the courses. The construction and design of these homes will match anything that the larger areas have to offer.

Bend also has a number of high hills which provide sites for some excellent view homes. Of course, there are some older and less expensive homes in the older part of the city that lend themselves to refurbishment. If one is looking for a small ranchette or perhaps even a larger ranch, then the Bend area can accommodate such a desire.

Housing is fairly expensive in Bend. The prices are competitive with those of the larger urban areas of western Oregon or Washington. A three bedroom/two bath home in Bend will start in the low $100,000s and go up. The larger new homes on golf courses or with views will range from $300,000 and up. Small ranchettes start in the mid $100,000 and if a person wants a big ranch they can be found in the million dollar range. The areas surrounding Bend, with the exception of Sisters, will generally have lower real estate prices.

Sunriver which is 15 miles to the south also provides fine housing opportunities. It is somewhat higher than Bend's 3,600 feet. This means that the winters are just a trifle bit colder. Sunriver is a very popular resort and residential community.

Bend is a city with modern services. The police and fire departments are staffed with paid professionals. The fire department staffing is supplemented with volunteers but the bulk of the personnel are full-time officers. Bend has the 911 system. Ambulance and emergency medical personnel are available when needed. The hospital, St. Charles Medical Center, is modern and comprehensive in its services. This hospital is a regional medical center for Central Oregon. It has 181 beds and is expanding. The hospital is one of the many features that draws people to Bend.

Bend schools are well thought of throughout Oregon. The District's enrollment is around 11,000, which allows it to provide a strong program. Central Oregon Community College provides for some of the higher education needs of the community. Extension courses are also available from several of Oregon's four-year institutions. The Redmond airport, 16 miles to the north, provides for commercial air service.

Culturally, Bend has a large number of opportunities. There are two excellent amateur theater groups which treat the town folks to some very professional performances. The Deschutes County Library along with the College library provide a superior library collection. There are a number of first class music festivals held each year in the community. There are numerous art galleries and museums. The College also contributes to the cultural and entertainment environment of the community.

Recreation is a big industry in Bend. The outdoors is the main focus. Mt. Bachelor and the smaller Hoodoo ski area provide for excellent downhill skiing. Bachelor is considered one of the premier ski areas in the United States. It has a 3,100 foot drop and a number of modern lifts. If a person wants skiing, then Mt. Bachelor is among the best. One will also find excellent cross country skiing, snowshoeing and snowmobiling in the Central Oregon area. Fishing is good with over 150 lakes and miles and miles of some of the best stream fishing in the West. These streams also provides some thrilling moments for the whitewater rafting enthusiast.

A person has never really lived until they have seen the snow-capped Three Sisters peaks (Hope, Faith and Charity). These mountains along with the rest of the Cascade Range provide for backpacking, climbing, horseback packing, camping, hunting and just the peaceful solitude for which so many of us hunger. Smith Rock is also nearby and people from all over the West come to these cliffs to test themselves as accomplished rock climbers. For those who like to hit the little white ball around a green pasture, there are a number of very fine golf courses in the Bend vicinity. If a person is a gardener then take note, the growing season is a short 92 days.

Bend is 160 miles southeast of Portland and 128 miles east of Eugene. Redmond and nearby Sisters, the other two communities in the Central Oregon triangle are only 20-30 minutes away.

Summary: Bend is a wonderful place for those folks who want an active lifestyle. The climate is invigorating and the scenery is awe inspiring. The services are first rate and St. Charles Medical Center does not take a back seat to any hospital. Bend is a good place to raise children, the educational services are excellent and there is a lot for young folks to do. Housing is a bit high but one has to realize the desirability of Bend. Perhaps the worst thing about Bend is the fact that a busy highway passes right through the center of town. Work is underway to partially alleviate the situation. Don't be mislead, the traffic impact is limited to a few streets. One or two blocks either side of the highway one will find the tranquility expected in a beautiful city in Central Oregon.

Klamath Falls (18,000 Pop.)

There is an old saying that one should never judge a book by its cover. That saying applies to Klamath Falls. As one passes through KF (Klamath Falls) one is hardly impressed. KF is more than just a city of 18,000 people on Highway 97. It is a city that is the commercial and cultural focus of a large rural area which takes in large portions of Northern California and Southern Oregon.

The KF area has some great scenery, cultural opportunities, recreation and good real estate values. It is high desert, located close to the mountains, and at the base of the giant Upper Klamath Lake. Majestic Mt. Shasta looms up on the horizon to the south.

The cost of living is below the national average. The economy is stable and is supported by the railroad, agriculture, tourism and the wood product industry. Government agencies also play an important role in the economic picture as does Kingsley Air Force Base.

The wood products industry has felt the impact of government regulations regarding logging in national forests but logging still is important. A drought of several years ago impacted the water supply but not to the point that it is a critical factor, yet. The community sees the current condition as a warning and is taking steps to conserve and improve the water supply.

The older sections of the city are on the valley floor and the newer homes are on the outskirts and on the hills to the north and east of town. A three bedroom/two bath home can be purchased for less than $100,000. Land and homes on the rivers of the area start in the high $100,000 range and go up from there. A nice view home can be purchased for

Oregon

$150,000 and up. Golf course homes will start at $200,000. One thing that is unique to the KF area is the use of geothermal heat for heating homes and businesses.

Police services are provided by a paid staff. The fire service personnel are also paid with some volunteer support. The city and county have a cooperative fire protection system. Medically, the community is served by Merle West Medical Center, a 130 bed facility. 911 service is available.

There are two school systems, city and county. The city system has an enrollment of 4,000 pupils, while the county provides services to 6,000 pupils. The test scores of the students are above the national average. The Oregon Institute of Technology is located in KF. It is an outstanding technical college and has a student enrollment of 2,300.

Klamath Falls International Airport provides for air transportation. Horizon Air operates in this area. The Air National Guard operates out of Kingsley Air Force Base and every once in awhile a person can catch a quick glimpse of a F16 flashing by.

Klamath Falls has a good cultural climate with theater, art galleries and museums, a symphony and choral groups. Unique to this area are Favell Museum with its large collection of Indian artifacts and Western art, and Klamath Wildlife Gallery, which is devoted to paintings of animal and Western plants. The Riverhouse Gallery features only Klamath Basin artists and specializes in a Native American theme.

Klamath Falls has a renovated performing arts center that seats 800. This is the only one in Southeastern Oregon and Northern California. It is the home of a number of plays and musicals put on by the Linkville Players. It is also the home of the KF symphony and the community's choral groups.

Being located next to the mountains and at the base of one of the largest bodies of fresh water in the Northwest, makes for an abundance of recreational opportunities. Fishing is a big interest in the area, as is hunting. Downhill skiing is within a reasonable distance at Mt. Bachelor, Mt. Shasta and Mt. Ashland. There are plenty snowmobiling and cross country skiing opportunities. Of course, with the mountains and large expanses of hills, rivers and lakes; backpacking, horseback riding and camping are very popular. Golfing is great in the spring, summer and falls. The Klamath Basin is in the direct migratory path of the Canadian (Honker) Geese and many other birds, as they wind their way north and south as the seasons change. The magnificent Bald Eagle winters in the Basin. Bird watching is very rewarding in this area.

Klamath Falls is not close to any of the larger urban areas. Medford is over the mountains and 76 miles to the west. Bend is 137 miles up Highway 97 to the north. Eugene is 173 miles and Portland 279 miles in distance. The mountains of the regions make winter travel a challenge at times.

Summary: Despite its isolation from the larger urban areas, Klamath Falls has a lot to offer. It has a healthy economy, a good cultural environment, plenty of recreational opportunities, pleasant climate, good community services and good real estate prices. The town is older and as such doesn't have the sparkle one might like but renovation is going on which is helping.

KF is a place where kids can grow and families can experience a good active life. The Western ethic is alive and well in Klamath Falls. Don't drive through without looking it over.

Northeastern Oregon

Northeastern Oregon has some of the most beautiful and rugged lands in the United States. The Blue and Wallowa mountains provide forests, lakes, streams and rolling foothills covered with the golds and greens of crops. Cattle, horses, sheep and a scattering of llamas dot the hillsides of the rich valleys. This is a region where one can also find expanses of sagebrush and bunch grass much as it was found when those on the Oregon Trail trudged their way across this land. Perhaps the most rugged landscape is the great canyon called Hell's Canyon. The Snake River twists and churns its way along the bottom of this 7,000 foot deep gorge and finally, some miles later, empties into the gigantic Columbia River. Variety certainly describes the land mass of Northeastern Oregon.

The towns are small and located, for the most part, in the rich valleys. Agriculture, wood products, and tourism provide the foundation for the area's economy. There are some travel trailer manufacturing companies located in the region. The cost of living is generally below the national average.

The people are hard working and friendly. For recreation they lean toward the outdoor adventures found in fishing, hunting, hiking, whitewater rafting, boating, off road motoring, downhill skiing, snowmobiling, and cross country skiing.

This is an area where the "Stetson" hat is common place and high-heeled cowboy boots fit right in. A pickup truck, and there are hundreds, will have a gun rack which will carry a gun in the fall and a fishing rod in the spring and summer.

The school districts are small but adequate and the achievement is usually above the national average. Because these school districts are hundreds of square miles, bussing is prevalent in the outlying areas. Children are usually brought to a central school facility. Eastern Oregon State University, the only four year institution east of the Oregon Cascades, Blue Mountain Community College and Walla Walla Community College provide for the bulk of the higher education opportunities in the region.

Each city has a paid police force and volunteers usually make up the bulk of fire personnel. Boise and Walla Walla provide hospital services for those needing specialized treatment. The towns provide small hospitals very capable of providing services for most of the medical problems that confront a population. 911 is available and fire personnel are trained in emergency medical procedures. Medical airlift services are also available.

The climate is warm in the summer and cold in the winter. The summers are dry with warm days and cool evenings. In the winter the snow is deep in the mountains and lighter in the valleys. The falls are pleasantly warm and the valleys are full of color. The springs are a welcome relief from the winter chills.

Culturally, one is surprised with the abundance of events. Symphony concerts, choir presentations, opera, magnificent art shows, museums, lecture series, dramatic and musical productions are all there. The University has several theaters capable of hosting professional performances. The people of the West are use to traveling for their entertainment and so each community has something to offer and the other communities come to enjoy the productions.

This area of Oregon, like many others, is getting to be the home of many artists and writers. Historically, the Oregon Trail and the Nez Perce Indians receive the bulk of attention.

Real estate is about as reasonable as one will find any place in the Northwest. Some communities have a scarcity of contemporary housing but remodeling and new construction are always possible. Small ranchettes are available, as are very large ranches. View property is certainly plentiful.

Water is always a concern in the dryer areas of the West. The valleys in this area appear to be adequately supplied but the folks are always watchful for situations that might threaten their water supply.

The region is somewhat isolated from larger urban communities. Roads are good, air travel is by private aircraft or by traveling to a place like Boise or Walla Walla for commercial flights. One should understand that these small communities pride themselves on being self-sufficient. Their reliance on larger urban areas comes down to specialized medical procedures, an occasional shopping junket, commercial air service or a weekend for entertainment.

If one is looking for a place where they can enjoy the great outdoors, have variety in the landscape and get away from the rush of the large city, then one should definitely take a look at Northeastern Oregon.

The following communities were visited: Enterprise, La Grande and Baker City.

Enterprise (1,900 Pop.)

Enterprise, the largest community in Wallowa County and the county seat, is in a valley of golden fields, rich brown soil, handsome cabins, neat farms, lakes and the evergreen forest. There are fast flowing rivers, deep (really deep) canyons and towering mountains in Wallowa County. This section of Oregon is often referred to as "The Switzerland of America".

Oregon

This is a valley where catalog ordering is hail and hearty. It is a community that artists have taken a liking to and their influence is very obvious.

As for the population of Wallowa County, 56 % of the folks are clustered in three communities—Wallowa, Enterprise and Joseph. This leaves a little more than 3,000 people spread out over the remaining 3,100 mile square miles of the county. There are places, as is true for many parts of the Northwest, where neighbors can be a number of miles away.

The 364,000 acre Eagle Cap Wilderness area is located here The steepest passenger gondola in the United States scales the sides of the 8,200 foot Mt. Howard. Beautiful Lake Wallowa rests in the bowl created by bygone glaciers. The delicious land locked salmon scoot about the lake looking for a fisherman's lure. One must not forget Hell's Canyon on the Snake River. This is a canyon that is wild, rugged and awesome.

One thing a person can say about this part of the country is that it is big—big mountains, big lakes, big forest, a big river and a big canyon.

Enterprise's economy is supported by agriculture (cattle, hay and grains), wood products and tourism. The growing season is 80 days and so if a person wants to raise palm trees this is definitely not the place.

There is something unique about Enterprise and nearby Joseph, they both have bronze foundries. The artistic work these foundries do is fabulous. If a person enjoys the metal sculptures of Remington then it is a sure thing that the similar works of these foundries will be popular.

A new three bedroom/two bath home with a view can be purchased in the mid $100,000 range. An older house, of the same size, can be found in the $80,000 to a low $100,000 range. A parcel of several acres, with a three bedroom and two bath house, can be found in the mid $100,000 range. Construction usually focuses on custom work and remodeling.

The police department is staffed with paid employees and the fire services are provided by volunteers. The hospital is called Wallowa Memorial. It is small but able to handle most routine care. Walla Walla and Boise hospitals offer support for the more severe cases. 911 is available.

Oregon

This is a rural area and the schools reflect that fact in that they will be small and students will be bussed from the countryside. Higher education is provided by Eastern Oregon State University and Blue Mountain Community College in Pendleton.

There are airports in Enterprise and Joseph. These facilities serve private aircraft. Commercial air service is located in Boise or Walla Walla.

Culturally, Enterprise and the surrounding towns are drawing a number of artists and crafts persons. Local art is readily available and from the layman's perspective it is quite pleasing. There are a number of community affairs such as the Chief Joseph Days, art festivals, a jazz festival, a classic car show, a writers' conference and the Alpenfest with its yodeling, dancing, crafts, food and beer.

Recreation is focused on the outdoors. Mountain climbing, fishing, windsurfing, boating, hunting, downhill and cross country skiing, snowmobiling, camping, hiking, backpacking and so on. If one chooses, a person will never be without an opportunity for some type of wholesome adventure in this "Switzerland".

This area is somewhat isolated and that might be one of its appealing features to those who long for the simpler life. La Grande is 67 mile to the southwest and Pendleton is 117 miles to the west. Walla Walla is about 155 mile to the northwest.

Summary: If one is looking for "Switzerland in America" then the Enterprise area is it. The valley is protected by the mountains and so the weather is reasonable. The summers are a delight and the winters are our fantasies come true. The air is clear and the scenery is breathtaking. It is a rural area and so a certain amount of self sufficiency is desirable. The services are adequate and the crime rate is low. In the winter it is a great place to have a snug little home, a giant fireplace, a good book and lots of hot coffee or chocolate. In the summer a porch swing and lots of lemonade will do nicely. If that's not enough then a fishing rod, a cool stream and a big trout might suit your fancy. This is a great place and be sure to give it a "look-see".

La Grande (12,000 Pop.)

La Grande is a small university town in a splendid valley among the mountains of northeastern Oregon. Almost one half of the 26,000 people living in Union County reside in La Grande. The Grande Ronde River flows through the 20 mile long valley. This area is often referred to as the "Valley of Peace" and that is definitely the feeling that exists there. La Grande, like Baker City, is located on the old Oregon Trail. Remnants of the trail still exist to this day. The valley is nestled between the Eagle Cap Wilderness region and the Elkhorn Ridge. The valley floor is taken up with agriculture and the hillsides and the mountains have large forests.

The economy is supported with agriculture, wood products, the university and travel trailer construction. Boise Cascade, a large wood products company, and Fleetwood, a travel trailer company, are both located in La Grande. The agricultural scene is concerned with grains, fruits, vegetable, cattle, sheep, horses and llamas. As the area grows, water becomes an increasing concern. Any shortage of water is very detrimental to the agricultural activities. Consequently, a "sharp-eye" is kept on the areas water supply.

La Grande is the commercial center for much of the surrounding region. This community has had some success in attracting several manufacturing firms and are aggressively seeking other such firms. There are several industrial parks available in this wonderful little town.

An older three bedroom/two bath home can be found for $95,000. A new home of similar size will range from $100,000 into the $120,000s. View homes will range from $125,000 up to the $300,000s. Five acres with a 2,000 square foot house will cost in the neighborhood of $200,000.

The police and fire services are staffed with paid professionals, with the fire personnel supported by volunteers. 911 is available. The Grande Ronde Hospital is nationally recognized as one of the 100 top hospitals in the United States. It is a facility of 84 beds. Support for specialized treatment is provided by Boise and Walla Walla hospitals.

The school district has an enrollment of about 2,800 students. The students achievement scores are high. Eastern

Oregon

Oregon State University is located in La Grande. It is not only responsible for providing for higher education in this remote Oregon region but it also adds to the cultural opportunities in the region.

There is an airport in La Grande that has a hard surfaced, 8,000 foot runway. The U.S. Forest Service keeps it DC4's at this airport. These aircraft are used for forest fire control. The airport also accepts private aircraft but there are no commercial flights. Boise is the closest place where major commercial passenger service is available.

When it comes to cultural and entertainment events, La Grande has a wide variety of offerings. The University's Mary Jane Loso Hall has two modern theaters and an attractive art gallery. This Hall is home to the McKensie Theater which seats 450 and is suitable for major productions. The "No Name" Theater seats 125 and handles small productions. The Nightingale Art Gallery, also part of the Hall, exhibits art from throughout Oregon and produces some outstanding art shows.

Up the road from La Grande is the Elgin Opera House which is quartered in the restored 80 year old City Hall. It provides some splendid productions. In addition to the above, there are barbershop quartets, a community symphony and choir. All in all, the cultural climate of the community is very good.

La Grande, like close by Enterprise and Baker City, is recreationally oriented toward the outdoors. The rivers, lakes and mountains provide numerous opportunities to enjoy what nature has provided. The falls provides opportunities for big game hunting. In the colder months there is downhill skiing at Spout Springs or Anthony Lakes. The mountains and the hills provide opportunities for snowmobiling and cross country skiing. In the warmer months camping, hiking, biking, backpacking, horseback riding, fishing, boating, whitewater rafting, off road motoring, rock climbing, hang gliding, golf and any number of other activities are possible. Needless to say one is never without something to do in the great outdoors when they are in La Grande - and there are no crowds.

Pendleton is 44 miles to the west and Walla Walla is only 88 miles away. Boise is 175 miles to the east and Portland is 260 miles to the west.

Summary: La Grande is a pleasing rural community nestled in among some very lovely mountains. The town is blessed with a university that adds greatly to the cultural, recreational and educational environment of the community. Real estate is reasonable and the town is large enough to provide adequate services. The "Valley of Peace" is a good place to raise children and enjoy the less stressful life offered by a smaller community. It's on the main road through northeastern Oregon so be sure to drop by and give it some of your time.

Baker City (9,000 Pop.)

Baker City is located in a beautiful broad valley in the shadow of two magnificent mountain ranges, the Wallowas and Blues. The floor of the valley is covered with cattle ranches, both big and small. Certain portions of the valley are still unimproved semiarid land. Bunch grass and sage brush are right at home in this dry environment. As one approaches the mountains, pine trees and more lush meadows take over the landscape. The silvery Powder River winds its way through the valley and flows through Baker City.

The city, with its broad shaded streets and neat homes, is appealing to the eye and gives one the feeling that this would be a nice place to live. The business section is older, with broad sidewalks and turn-of-the-century store fronts. As one approaches the highways, the businesses show a more contemporary architectural influence. Growth is expected to continue in Baker City during the rest of the 90's at about the 4% rate.

The economy of the community is dominated by livestock production, wood products, cement and tourism. Electricity price are some of the lowest in the nation. Since the area relies upon irrigation for growing crops, the water supply is always a concern. Baker City's water supply appears to be adequate for the foreseeable future—a strong asset for the future growth of the area.

Oregon

Real estate prices are very reasonable in the area. A newer three bedroom/two bath home can be found in the lower $100,000s. Older homes of similar size can be found in the $60,000 to $90,000 range. Housing is not overly abundant but homes that can be remodeled are available. Land is relatively inexpensive, with an acre price ranging from $850 to $2000. Of course, the lower the price the less desirable the land.

Baker City has a paid police staff and the fire protection is provided by a small nucleus of paid staff supported with volunteers. Emergency medical technicians are available with the fire services. 911 services are available as well as Life Flight services.

Hospital care is provided by the 49 bed St. Elizabeth Hospital. Boise and Walla Walla hospitals support St. Elizabeth.

The schools are good with the students ranking above the national averages. The district enrolls about 2,400 student which allows it to offer a broad range of services. The district is large, over 1,100 square miles. Bus transportation is provided for outlying areas. Post high school education is provided by regional community colleges and Eastern Oregon State University in La Grande.

Commercial air service is available in Boise, approximately 128 miles to the east. Baker City has an airport which has a 5,100 foot runway and provides a wide range of services for private aircraft. No commercial service is available out of Baker City.

Culturally, this area has a rich historical heritage upon which it has capitalized. The Oregon Trail Interpretative Center is located on a hill overlooking Baker Valley. It is one of the most impressive displays of life on the trail. When people come out of the center they have a real appreciation for the courage and fortitude of our pioneer ancestors. It draws thousands of tourists to the area each year. Volunteers play a great part in welcoming the tourists and maintaining the displays.

As for entertainment, the folks of Baker rely on the schools, their own ingenuity, and the Crossroad Arts Council. They have the typical rodeos and community festivals associated with small western towns. Eastern Oregon State University with its cultural and entertainment productions is located in La Grande only 44 miles to the northwest.

Recreation for most of the folks in the Baker area revolves around the "great outdoors". One can downhill ski, cross country ski, snowmobile and ice fish in the winter. In the spring the fishing, hiking and camping are popular. In the summer the boating, fishing, backpacking, camping and horseback riding. Hunting is added to the list in the fall. It is, as is most of the Northwest, a place where one can really get back to nature. There are places where it would be entirely possible that the only other person to have visited that same place would have been an Indian brave of some ancient tribe, on the trail of a bull elk. Want to get away from big city life, then this is the place.

Baker City is located on Interstate 84 which is a good highway and carries most of the traffic from Washington and Oregon bound for Boise and Salt Lake City. The area is some distance from larger urban centers. Boise is 128 miles to the east, Seattle is 400 miles and Portland is 304. Walla Walla is 141 to the northwest. Even though it is somewhat isolated, the community is fairly self sufficient.

Summary: Baker City and the surrounding area is a wonderful place to experience the relaxed and peaceful life offered by a beautiful western valley nestled among magnificent mountains. It is a rural American community, a great place to raise kids with lots of healthful recreational opportunities. The schools are good, the services are very adequate, electrical power is priced with some of the lowest in the nation, the streets are safe and real estate prices are very reasonable. The people take pride in their community and they are friendly and caring. If this sounds like what you are looking for, take time to visit and talk to some of the folks. You won't be sorry.

Idaho Map

IDAHO (1,007,000 Pop.)

Idaho is a fabulous state! It is often referred to as the "Gem State". The name is quite appropriate considering that over 80 varieties of gemstone and large amounts of gold and silver deposits have been found. In addition to the minerals, the natural beauty of the state's vast forests, clear streams and rivers, numerous lakes, high mountains and deserts add credibility to the "Gem State" nickname.

The northern portion, called the Panhandle, is a region filled with mountains, forest, streams, rivers and lakes. Timber, mining and tourism with some agricultural pursuits provide the bulk of the income in the region. The Panhandle's commercial life is oriented toward the Inland Empire, an area that encompasses eastern Washington and northeastern Oregon. Spokane, in Washington, is the metropolitan focus of much of the Inland Empire and northern Idaho.

Central Idaho is composed of mountains, forest and exciting rivers. It has one of the largest primitive areas in the continental United States. This central region is also home to Hell's Canyon, the deepest gorge on the North American continent. This gorge is famous for its primitiveness, wildlife and splendid beauty.

Southern Idaho is somewhat different in its geographical features. There still are mountains, lakes, rivers and forests but a large part of the south is composed of semiarid lands. These lands, with the addition of water, have made southern Idaho a rich agricultural region. The scenery is less spectacular than in the north but certainly not devoid of some beautiful and inspiring gifts of nature.

In the eastern part of Southern Idaho there are some magnificent falls, some of the highest sand dunes in the United States and the entrance to West Yellowstone is nearby. The 160 square mile Bear Lake, on Idaho's southeastern border, is shared with Utah.

The southwestern part of Idaho is semiarid and, where water is available, great farms and ranches are prevalent. This region relies heavily on agriculture and commercial enterprises. Boise, the state capital, is a great commercial center where a number of large corporations have made their national and international headquarters.

Much of the weather of Idaho comes from the Pacific. The winters in the valleys are wet with some snow. Most of the snow falls in the higher elevations. This snow pack is a major factor in the plentifulness of water. The summers are hot, hotter in the south than in the north. Much of Idaho is protected from the extreme colds of the Canadian weather by the mountains.

The rivers of Idaho deliver large amounts of water to the state and other states down river. The Kootenai, Clark Fork, and Pend Oreille coupled with the Snake and Salmon rivers account for over 70 million acre feet of water annually. For comparison purposes the Colorado River carries from 12 to 15 million acre feet of water annually. In addition to water coming from surface streams and rivers, the Snake Plain Aquifer in southern Idaho provides the largest underground water flow on the North American continent.

Real estate prices, when compared to West coast prices, are very reasonable. This is a place where one can find small acreages, homes on lakes or in the mountains without spending an "arm and a leg".

The public schools are good. Idahoans have a strong work ethic and it is, for the most part, observable in the children. Since much of the area is rural, many children will find that they have to ride a bus to and from school. This is true in many parts of the Northwest and it doesn't seem to harm the children.

There are a number of colleges and universities that serve the people of Idaho. In the north and central part is the University of Idaho and Lewis and Clark State College. Also available for Idahoans are Washington State University, Whitworth College, Gonzaga University, and Eastern Washington University. In the south is Boise State University, Albertson College, Northwest Nazarene College and Idaho State University as well as colleges and universities in Montana and Utah.

With regard to medical services, each town has the ability to treat common types of problems. The larger communities provide more comprehensive medical care programs.

Many of the smaller communities are capable of transporting patients to regional medical centers via "Life Flight" services.

There are a number of larger cities that provide a vast array of cultural and entertainment opportunities for the various regions. Spokane and Coeur D'Alene in the north, Lewiston and Clarkston in the central portion and Boise, Pocatello and Idaho Falls in the south provide regional cultural and entertainment opportunities. That doesn't mean that the smaller towns are cultural "wastelands". They too add to the cultural and entertainment environment of the state.

As with much of the Northwest, Idaho's recreational activities center on the great outdoors. The mountains, lakes and rivers provide a recreational playground for its natives and visitors alike.

In closing there is one thing one should know about this great state's taxes. According to the *Kiplinger Personal Finance Magazine*, August 1995, pp. 58-59, Idaho's local and state tax load ranked seventh highest in the nation. Probably the consequence of having a large state and a small population. Many feel that Idaho's beauty and grandeur more than offset its tax position.

Panhandle

The Panhandle is an extension of the lower half of Idaho that extends northward toward Canada. It is a pleasant mountainous area with nice valleys that have beautiful lakes and rivers. There are numerous spots where a person can get away and just enjoy the beautiful surroundings and solitude afforded by the mountains and rivers. Lake Pend Oreille (pronounced Ponderay), Priest Lake, and Lake Coeur D'Alene are located in this region and are popular recreational destinations. These lakes are very large but there are a number of wonderful lesser lakes which are beautiful too. They are not overly crowded with people and are great places for a cozy little hideaway cabin.

The Clark Fork, Pend Oreille and the Kootenai rivers are the main rivers. They provide waterfronts for cabins and the fishing and boating is fabulous.

The Panhandle has a number of downhill ski areas and many are rated as among the best in the nation, Schweitzer and Silver Mountains for example. Besides downhill skiing, there is cross country skiing, snowmobiling, ice fishing, hunting, fishing, camping, hiking, mountain climbing, sailing and many other activities that are associated with this kind of region.

As for the economy, timber and wood products, agriculture and tourism are important income producers. Real estate prices are quite reasonable when compared to the large urban areas of western Washington and Oregon.

Education is considered good. Close-by opportunities for higher education are limited but there are fine institutions within a one or two hour drive for most of the communities. The smaller communities can provide for most medical services. Coeur D'Alene and Spokane are within a reasonable distance and can provide specialized medical services.

Culturally, the region relies upon "home town" kind of activities. More sophisticated and professional programs appear in the larger towns of Sandpoint and Coeur D'Alene. Spokane, one of the larger metropolitan communities in the Northwest, provides many of the cultural and entertainment events enjoyed by the folks of the Panhandle.

Commercial commuter air service flies out of Coeur D'Alene. The Spokane International Airport is the major national and international terminal of the region.

Bonners Ferry (2,200 Pop.)

The town was named after Edward Bonner who built the first ferry across the Kootenai River in the mid 1860's. Bonners Ferry is a small town in the northern part of the Idaho Panhandle. It is located in a broad fertile valley. Canada is just a few miles north. To the south and east are the Cabinets and Purcell mountains and the state of Montana.

To the west of the Valley are the rugged Selkirk Mountains. The beautiful Kootenai River winds its way through the valley. This is a region that is ideal for the person who wants some acreage for farming, raising horses and cattle or for just

Idaho

the sheer pleasure of getting up in the morning and enjoying the sights and sounds of a magnificent western valley.

Bonners Ferry has a population slightly over 2,000, while the sparsely populated Boundary County has around 9,000 residents. That works out to about 6 - 7 people per square mile for the county.

Timber has always been an important influence on the local economy. This industry, for the last 10 years or so, has been slower than in the past but it is still very important to the economy of the area. Agriculture is also very important. Cattle, grains, tree nurseries and hops are the major cash crops. Tourism is building.

Real estate prices in Bonners Ferry appeared to be quite reasonable. The area is very desirable for the individual who "hankers" for a more rural setting. A new three bedroom/two bath house will cost in the neighborhood of $85,000 and up. A three bedroom/two bath home with a small amount of land (1-10 acres) will cost in the low to mid $100,000s. Depending on the location, use and utilities, land will start at $1,200 per acre. Lots on the Kootenai River will range from $12,000 to $24,000.

The city provides a seven officer police force and fire protection is provided by volunteers. 911 service is available. A small community hospital is located there and the ambulance service is provided by volunteers. The city owns and operates its own hydroelectric plant on the Moyie River. This allows the community to provide rates that are some of the lowest in the West.

Public education is provided by a county system. There are five elementary schools and one high school. Enrollment is between 1,700 and 1,800 pupils. Post high school education is available through extension courses and/or by attending some of the institutions of higher learning to the south, i.e., Coeur d'Alene or in Washington state.

There is an airfield with a 4,000 foot runway. Commuter service is available. Spokane, 109 miles to the southwest, is the nearest national and international airport.

This is definitely a four season area. The winters are cold but zero is not often reached. Summers are warm with only a few days reaching temperatures over 90 degrees. The humidity is not uncomfortable. The precipitation usually runs around 24 inches per year. The heaviest snow falls usually starts in late December.

This area is a paradise for the outdoor enthusiast. There are opportunities for boating, fishing, camping, hiking, cross-country skiing, downhill skiing, snowmobiling, and hunting. Big game hunting includes deer, elk, bear, and moose. The rarely seen grizzly bear and caribou are protected. Bird hunting is also very good in the valley.

Of course, like all small communities, Bonners Ferry has its festivals and celebrations. The Winter Sports Festival, Spring Training Horse Show, Lions Club Fishing Derby, Kootenai River Days, Great Llama Challenge and Show, rodeo and Scandinavian Smorgasbord are all good examples.

Bonners Ferry is less than 30 miles from the Canadian border. Coeur d'Alene is 79 miles to the south and Spokane is 109 miles to the southwest. Bonners Ferry is somewhat isolated but according to Western standards, not so much as to be bothersome.

Summary: Bonners Ferry is a small rural community that looks to timber and agriculture for its economy. It has a definite four season year. A person who wants to experience the outdoors and the slower pace offered by the rural community will delight in the region around Bonners Ferry. Real estate is relatively inexpensive. Hunting and fishing are good. This area is a prime example of the beauty of a western mountain and valley setting.

Sandpoint (5,500 Pop.)

Sandpoint is a very popular area for the people of the Northwest. It is located in the Idaho Panhandle on the shores of Idaho's largest lake. Lake Pend Oreille, the main natural feature of the area, is very deep, 43 miles long, 6 miles wide with 111 miles of shoreline. The beautiful Selkirk Mountains are to the west of the lake and the Cabinet Mountains are to the east. The town is on the northwest shoreline of the lake. It is a busy little town that gives the appearance of great vitality.

Idaho

The lake receives much of a visitors attention but not to be overlooked are the two magnificent rivers that feed and drain the lake. The Clark Fork River, to the east, flows through a valley with rolling green hills, an occasional farm, and considerable scenic riverside property. The Pend Oreille River flows out of the big lake, west toward the town of Priest River and finally joins the Columbia River near the U.S./Canadian border. These rivers are ideal for a summer home or a permanent residence where one can enjoy an invigorating and refreshing four season environment.

Wood products, although less of an impact now than in the past, are still very important to the basic economy of Sandpoint. With the lake, mountains and Schweitzer Mountain Resort, tourism has developed into a substantial portion of the economy. Schweitzer alone accounts for bringing over 175,000 skiers to the area annually. Light industry is helping to diversify the economy and Sandpoint, like other smaller communities, is always on the lookout for businesses that will broaden the economic base.

A newer three bedroom/two bath home can be purchased in the low $100,000s and up. Similar homes on small acreages start in the upper $100,000s. View homes generally start in the mid $100,000s and go up quickly. Waterfront homes on the lake are generally quite expensive, starting in the neighborhood of the upper $200,000s. Waterfront footage goes for about $1,200 up to $2,000 per foot for prime locations.

Homes on the Pend Oreille River will cost about the same as lake frontage. The Clark Fork River has less expensive waterfront. Lots in the Sandpoint area will vary considerably depending on the location. A buildable lot can be found in the high $20,000s and up, while lake front lots will range from $100,000 to $200,000. Less expensive lake front lots can be found on the numerous smaller lakes in the area.

Also, there are some real estate opportunities afforded by Schweitzer Mountain Resort. This area is developing home sites and condos that make for excellent recreational investments. A beautiful four bedroom and three bath townhouse, at the village, will sell in the low $200,000. Partnerships are being promoted where two or more partners can buy into a townhouse. There are a variety of housing options which range from one bedroom condos to three or four bedroom and four bath townhouses. Some of the larger townhouses are priced in the mid $300,000s.

The Sandpoint Chamber of Commerce sponsors a plan center. The center provides a place where an individual's house plans can be reviewed by local contractors so they can bid on building. This center is a real convenience for the newcomer to the community who wants to build a house.

The police and fire services of Sandpoint are staffed with paid employees. The fire service relies on some volunteers. The Bonner Medical Center is an accredited, full-service hospital with 62 beds. Helicopter transportation is available to take patients, who need highly specialized care, to larger medical centers in Coeur D'Alene or Spokane. 911 service is available.

The local public school district is a county system. The county has 32,000 citizens and the school district serves about 5,800 youths in grades K-12. The community's support of its schools is evidenced by approval of a recent levy to build some new schools. North Idaho College, a community college, whose main campus is in Coeur D'Alene, also serves Sandpoint. The University of Idaho and Lewis and Clark State College offers extension classes.

There are a number of cultural pursuits available in the Sandpoint area. Theater and musical pursuits are alive and well. The two-month long Festival at Sandpoint provides programs that draw national talent like Willie Nelson, Preservation Hall Jazz Band, Maureen McGovern, and the Spokane Symphony. In addition, other activities such as the International Draft Horse Show, Music on the Mountain and Schweitzer International Music Camp, add to the community's festivities. All in all, the programs show sophistication and creativity.

Snowmobiling, cross country and downhill skiing, ice skating and fishing are all available in the winter. Schweitzer Mountain Resort is a destination ski resort that has powder snow and up-to-date equipment and facilities. In the summer, the focus turns to the lakes and rivers. Boating, water skiing, sailing, swimming, fishing, hiking and golf are available. In the fall, hunting takes the lead and the hunts are for deer, elk and, sometimes, bear.

Idaho

Sandpoint has four seasons. The summers are not extremely hot and the winters are not unbearably cold. The precipitation is about 32 inches each year and the snow amounts to about 65 inches, with most of it coming in December and January. The prevailing weather comes from the west.

Sandpoint is on three major railroads and has passenger service to points west and east. Seattle, by highway, is 350 miles to the west and Spokane is 80 miles to the southwest. Coeur D'Alene is 45 miles to the south and Missoula is 200 miles to the east.

Private air transportation is available from the Sandpoint General Aviation Airport. It has a 4,200 foot runway and is expecting instrumentation capabilities soon. Commercial commuter air service is available at Coeur D'Alene and national and international air service is available at Spokane.

Summary: Sandpoint is a good compromise between the suburban/urban areas and the rural area. It is large enough to have the readily available services many of us have grown to expect. It is in a beautiful location with mountains, lakes and rivers. Outdoor activities are numerous and the four seasons allow variety. The community has a wide scope of cultural activities. The weather is very pleasant for the majority of time. Accessibility is fairly good with larger urban areas within 50 - 100 miles. This is a town that people have found to be a delightful place to live.

Coeur d'Alene (27,000 Pop.)

Idaho has many "gems" and undoubtedly one of the most beautiful is the magnificent lake called Coeur d'Alene. This lake has been dubbed by the *National Geographic Magazine* as one of the world's ten most beautiful lakes. The lake is approximately 25 miles long and has 135 miles of shoreline. If a person likes water, then Coeur d'Alene is the place with over 60 bodies of water within 60 miles. This region is covered with forested mountains, crystal clear lakes and rivers, neat valley farms, the city of Coeur d'Alene and a number of smaller towns.

Idaho

The economy of Coeur d'Alene depends on wood products, tourism and agriculture. Mining is considerably less important than in the past. The largest employers are Hegadone Corporation in the hospitality industry, Advanced Input Devices making computer keyboards and the Kootenai Medical Center. Lumber and wood products, albeit less than in the past, play an important part in the prosperity of the community.

The hospitality industry is very important to the economic welfare of the city. Among the many unique features of this area is the Coeur d'Alene Resort. This facility has 328 hotel rooms, a convention center, a 6,000 plus yard golf course and a beautiful marina The hotel is an attractive high-rise building on carefully groomed grounds. The rooms are superb and the views are breathtaking. *Conde Nast Traveler* magazine selected the Coeur d'Alene Resort as America's top mainland resort. The Resort was rated perfect for service, atmosphere and location.

Agriculture is not to be forgotten as one of the important aspects of the community's economy. Grass seed production, wheat and barley are the main cash crops.

The growth experienced during the last 25 years has precipitated a strong construction industry. A new three bedroom/ two bath home can start in the low $100,000s. Larger homes on small acreage will run $200,000 and up. For example, a new home on five acres was found for $250,000. Lake, valley and mountain view homes will start in the mid $200,000 and go up quickly. Lakefront and lake view lots will start at $100,000 and up. Obviously, the closer to the lake and the better the view, the higher the price. Prices are climbing and it appears that the trend will continue.

Coeur d'Alene is a city of about 27,000 people. As such, it supports a paid police and fire department. The fire department's paid employees are backed up by volunteers.

The public K-12 school district is a good size with approximately 6,600 pupils. The district provides a secondary vocational-technical program. A post-secondary, vocational-technical program is provided by North Idaho College. It is a local community college and another community college, Spokane Community College, is located a short distance away in Spokane. There are a number of four-year institutions in nearby eastern Washington plus the University of Idaho in Moscow, Idaho.

Probably one of the strong points of the Coeur d'Alene area is the Kootenai Medical Center. This 187 bed center provides comprehensive medical treatment for much of the Idaho Panhandle. Nearby Spokane has several very large hospitals that augment the services provided by Kootenai.

In May 1995, the *Coeur d'Alene Press* ran a news article entitled, "Coeur d'Alene on Top 10 Places to Retire List." The essence of the article was that due to the high marks for leisure living, Coeur d'Alene was ranked seventh in the latest edition of "Retirement Places Rated" by MacMillan Travel.

The city is large enough to have a variety of cultural and entertainment opportunities. Lake City Playhouse, a community theater, is in operation year around. Festivals such as Art on the Green and Fred Murphy Days are held in the inviting city park. Other events are the Coeur d'Alene Marathon, the Sunday Concert Series, the Classic Car Show, Coeur d'Alene Summer Theater, the Northwest Summer Playhouse, fishing derbies, rodeos and the Coeur d'Alene Triathalon.

Somewhat unusual for this "neck of the woods" is the Coeur d'Alene Greyhound Park. It was opened in 1988 and has been going strong ever since. The crowds come from both the Washington and Idaho sides of the border to watch the dogs run.

Golf is popular and the half dozen excellent golf courses nearby make opportunities readily accessible. Lake Coeur d'Alene furnishes opportunities for fishing, boating, water skiing, paragliding and even golfing. The Coeur d'Alene Resort Golf Course has a floating golf green on the lake. Hunting and fishing are big in this area of lakes, rivers, forests and mountains. Hiking and camping in the summer are popular.

In the winter, attention turns to snow-type activities. Coeur d'Alene received accolades from *SKI Magazine* as "America's most livable ski town." The ski areas of Schweitzer, Silver Mountain, Lookout Pass and 49 North are all within 2 hours drive. Idaho snow is usually dry and plentiful. Of course, one can also find opportunities to snowmobile, cross country ski and snowshoe.

Idaho

Idaho is a wonderful place to prospect for precious minerals and gems. In fact, just south of Coeur d'Alene, at Emerald Creek, is a garnet digging area. In the Coeur d'Alene Mountains, gold and silver still await a lucky prospector.

The weather is relatively mild considering that Coeur d'Alene is in northern Idaho where one expects more severe weather. January, the coldest month, has an average daytime temperature of 34 degrees. The highest temperatures come in July and August with the average daytime temperatures in the mid 80s. The average rainfall is 26 inches and the snowfall is about 49 inches. The snowfall is spread over the period of November through March. The humidity in the summer is quite low which makes for pleasant heat.

Coeur d'Alene has very good accessibility. It is located on Interstate 90. Spokane is 32 miles to the west. Seattle is 6 hours to the west. Missoula, to the east, is 167 miles away. The Canadian border, with Sandpoint and Bonners Ferry in between, is slightly more than 100 miles to the north. It is 45 miles to Spokane International Airport. Coeur d'Alene has an airport that is capable of handling both commuter and private aircraft.

Summary: Coeur d'Alene is indeed a delightful community. It is a place where a person can be very comfortable. The cost of living is relatively low. There are a myriad of activities in which one can engage. The city has first rate health, educational and protection services. The proximity to a large urban area, Spokane, is very good. Housing is available and can fit the pocketbook of most buyers. Coeur d'Alene is indeed one of Idaho's "gems".

Central Idaho

Going south from the Panhandle, the state starts to widen and will be referred to as Central Idaho. It is the least populated region in the state. Most of its population is located on the western side of the state, near the Washington border.

The mighty Salmon River runs through this region. This is the river made famous in the movie called "The River of No Return". The Snake and the Clearwater rivers also supply water to this area. The Snake, famous for its Hell's Canyon, is the largest river in Idaho and is a major contributor to the Columbia system. The rivers in this part of Idaho have "white" waters that will challenge the most expert of rafters and kayakers. Fishing is spectacular on these rivers.

Timber, agriculture and tourism are the primary economic consideration in Central Idaho. Lewiston, Idaho and Clarkston, Washington are the largest communities in the region. For all practical purposes these two cities are one, separated by the Snake River and serving a total metropolitan population of about 38,000.

The public schools are good. There are a number of institutions of higher learning convenient to the west-side communities. Medical facilities in Lewiston and Clarkston are capable of handling most medical procedures. The large hospitals in Spokane augment the medical services of the region.

Lewiston has an airport that provides commuter services. Spokane International provides major commercial air services.

Lewiston and Clarkston (38,000 Pop.)

Where the magnificent Clearwater and Snake rivers join on their way to the mighty Columbia River, one finds the valley towns of Lewiston and Clarkston. The high hills that shelter the valley are brown and barren. They have a stark and primitive beauty that changes as the sun and clouds drift across the sky. Lewiston is a town of some 31,000 people and Clarkston's population is close to 7,000.

These communities serve as the "jumping off" place for some of the wildest and most primitive areas in North America: Hells Canyon, the Clearwater National Forest and the Frank Church and River of No Return wilderness areas. These primitive regions are where roads run out and trails take over. In these areas one can go days and perhaps weeks without seeing another person.

The economy of the region is mainly concerned with agriculture and wood products. Tourism, fiberglass jet boats, ammunition manufacturing, government agencies and port operations also add to the economic base of Lewiston and Clarkston.

There are three ports on the Snake River that serve the region. The Lewiston port handles containers, the Wilma port focuses on wood chips from the nearby mills and the Clarkston port serves cruise ships and loads logs. The barge traffic that comes to Lewiston and Clarkston is made possible by the eight interlocking reservoirs behind the dams on the Columbia and Snake rivers.

Lewiston and Clarkston form a regional commercial center. Unlike many older towns, the downtown of Lewiston is an inviting place with its quaint shops, slow traffic, broad sidewalks and gorgeous trees.

As with many Northwestern towns, the cost of electricity and the general cost of living is quite reasonable. It should be pointed out that because of the Idaho tax structure, the cost of living on the Washington side of the Snake River is slightly lower.

Real estate is reasonable. There are many sites which have great territorial views and homes in these areas can be found in the mid $100,000 and up. A new three bedroom/two bath home can be found in the low $100,000s. A home on a golf course will start in the low $200,000s and go up. Small acreages with a home can be found in the mid $100,000s.

Lewiston has a paid police and fire department. The smaller Clarkston has a paid city police department supported by the county sheriff's department. The Clarkston fire department is volunteer. A 911 service and Life Flight service is available for both communities.

There are three hospitals. St. Joseph's Regional Medical Center in Lewiston is the largest medical facility in the region. It is capable of handling the majority of illnesses. Cases needing highly specialized care are sent to Spokane hospitals. Tri-State Memorial Hospital, with 62 beds, provides normal hospital services and specializes in renal dialysis. The third hospital, River Crest, specializes in addiction and psychiatric services.

The public schools are good. Lewiston has an enrollment of 5,000 and Clarkston enrolls 3,100. Besides the normal K-12 programs they both provide alternative schools.

Idaho

Lewis and Clark State College is located in Lewiston and has an enrollment of over 3,300 students. This college offers both four and two year degrees. In addition to Lewis and Clark State College, Washington State University and the University of Idaho are nearby. Walla Walla Community College has a branch campus in Clarkston.

Empire, United Express and Horizon Air commuter airlines serve Lewiston and Clarkston out of the Lewiston Nez Perce County Airport. Spokane International is the closest airport for national and international connections.

Culturally, the two towns merge into one cultural and entertainment entity. There are a number of things with which a person can become involved. There is the civic theater, the Washington/Idaho Symphonic Orchestra, ballet, community concerts, the Lewiston Round Up, which is the 4th largest rodeo in the West, the Lewis and Clark Air Show, boat races on the river, the Lewis and Clark State College Artist Series and any number of sports and cultural opportunities at the nearby Washington and Idaho universities. All and all, for a relatively small community, the towns of Lewiston and Clarkston provide a nice selection of cultural and entertainment opportunities.

This central Idaho region is a virtual storehouse of recreational opportunities. It is located adjacent to the largest concentration of wilderness areas in the lower 48 states. The Snake and Salmon rivers allow a person, with the aid of a jet boat, to return to a land that is much as the pioneers and Indians found it years ago. Here a person can hunt and fish, whitewater raft, hike, camp, photograph animals, flowers and ancient petroglyphs, as well as watch the eagles gracefully glide far above the river on some unseen current of air. This is a place where the sounds of breezes in the trees and the call of a far off bird soothes the soul and make one sensitive to the beauty and pleasure of being nearer one's Creator.

If its skiing a person wants, there are seven fine ski areas within less than three hours. Snowmobiling and cross country skiing are also available. Fishing on the Snake and Clearwater is unmatched. Besides the trout, bass, salmon and steelhead there are the "Great White" sturgeons. Hunting for big game is good in this area and there are guides that know

Idaho

where these "big fellows" hang out. The game includes elk, mountain goats, big horn sheep, bear, cougar, and mule deer. Of course, all hunting is strictly monitored and controlled by the state.

For those who prefer less strenuous pursuits, there are four 18 hole golf courses. The green fees - prepare yourself - are $11-$15 for 18 holes. If a person likes baseball, Lewis and Clark State University hosts the NAIA College World Series.

The climate deserves some mention because it is not what one would expect. The winters are relatively mild in the valley. Snow is an infrequent visitor. The summers are warm and dry. The growing season is 200 days and the sun shines, on the average, 170 days a year. There are four seasons and the spring and fall are a delight.

Spokane is the closest large urban area, 108 miles to the north. Seattle is 307 miles to the northwest, and Portland is due west 334 miles.

Summary: The Lewiston and Clarkston area is a place where one could be quite comfortable. It is popular with retirees. The services are good, the cost of living and real estate prices are reasonable, the economy is stable, cultural and entertainment opportunities are plentiful, and exciting and rewarding recreational activities abound. This is a community where the pace is slower and the environment wholesome. A little bit isolated but that, perhaps, is one of its beauties.

McCall (2,600 Pop.)

Up in an Idaho mountain valley, one finds the small resort town of McCall. This is a picturesque community on the shores of Payette Lake. Here one is greeted with magnificent pine trees, sparkling blue water and clear skies, clean air and refreshing breezes. This large lake provides for summer fishing, boating, sailing, swimming and water skiing. In the winter it freezes and ice fishing is in vogue.

McCall is becoming popular, not only as a resort, but also as a very desirable place to live full time. The population is normally around 2,600 but during the summer tourist season it can reach 15,000.

Idaho

The economy is supported by tourism, agriculture and forest products. McCall is also a home base to U.S. Forest Service smoke jumpers. Unemployment is relatively low in August, the height of the tourist season, but considerably higher in the winter.

McCall has become an attractive vacation spot for folks who live in Boise. Nearby Brundage Mountain is a popular destination ski facility. The snow is dry in this part of Idaho and there is lots of it. In addition to Brundage, Payette Lake and the Payette and Salmon rivers are attractions popular with tourists.

Real estate prices are reasonable for such an attractive spot. A new three bedroom/two bath home will cost in the mid $100,000 range. Homes on the golf course will range from the low $200,000s and up. There are a number of new developments going in and the vacant lots are reasonable - from $35,000 and up. Homes on small acreage can be found in the mid $100,000 and up. Lake front condos can be purchased for as low as $200,000. Prior to building in the area, it would be prudent to check on the availability of water and sewer services. At the time of this writing, the community was experiencing some difficulty in keeping up with the growth. They were working on the problem and felt that these services would be strengthened in the near future.

Police and fire services are a mixture of paid professionals and volunteers. The crime rate is low. McCall Memorial Hospital, although small, is very adequate for most of the services needed. Critical cases or cases needing special procedures are sent to Boise. 911 is available and Life Flight services are there for emergencies.

The public school district is small, 1,300 enrollment, but capable of providing a good educational program. A strong college preparatory program is offered but the vocational program is limited. Test scores are generally well above the national averages. Boise State University and the University of Idaho offer adult and college credit classes in the community.

McCall has an airport that can handle private aircraft. Operating out of the airport are several air charters that specialize in "back country" flights for those who want to hunt and/or fish in the wilderness.

Much of the culture of the community is depicted in its celebrations. The McCall Frontier Day Rodeo captures the robust nature of the community's past and present. The Summer Festival, a musical production, provides a more sophisticated reflection of the community. The Valley County Fair reminds the residents of the more basic and simple rural lifestyle. The Triathalon exhibits the strength of the community. Finally, the Winter Carnival, with its huge ice sculptures, demonstrates the creativeness of the folks in McCall. In addition to the above, the community supports a community chamber orchestra, a ballet school, a playhouse and a number of very fine art galleries.

Recreation is the "king" in this valley. Skiing at Brundage is about as good as it gets and the lift tickets are still reasonable. There are literally hundreds of lakes in the region that provide for water sports and fishing. The rivers will gladly provide a wild ride that makes one quickly learn to respect the power of these rivers. The mountains have everything from hunting, climbing, hiking and camping to offer. The town offers tennis, golf, ice skating and a slower pace for those who just like to laze around, read a good book or perhaps just take in the beautiful scenery.

The summer temperatures range, on the average, from the 70s in the day to the 40s in the night. In the winters the averages range from the 30s to the low teens, with about 20 days of zero or below. Precipitation averages about 28 inches per year with a large portion being in the form of snow—about 60 inches. The growing season is short—69 days.

How does one get to this wonderful place? Leave Boise on highway 55 and go north for about three hours and you will come to a beautiful lake and a charming town—that's McCall.

Summary: For someone who loves the outdoors and lots of activity, then McCall is just right. The services are adequate, the schools are small but good. The community is a wholesome place to live and raise children. It can get somewhat crowded in the summer but that just makes for some wonderful people watching opportunities. Real estate was not particularly expensive and certainly the scenic beauty of the area is beyond reproach. The summers are delightful and the winters are just right for winter sports.

Southern Idaho

In Southern Idaho one notices a transformation from the mountainous to the semiarid. For purposes of discussion, the southern part of Idaho starts where the state widens on the map.

The mountains are still present in a large part of the south. The Sawtooth Mountains are beautiful and rugged. This is the home of Sun Valley, famous for its destination resorts. The Salmon River dips into this area and provides many a thrill on its "white" waters. Yes, the fishing is still great. Farther south and to the east one will run into the Shoshone Falls, Craters of the Moon and the giant Bear Lake and more mountains. To the west is the state capital, Boise, lots of farm land, sand dunes, vineyards and the southern beginning of Hell's Canyon. The Snake River traverses the whole southern part of the state. Southern Idaho is the driest part of the state. Irrigation is prevalent and the Snake Plain Aquifer and the Snake River provide a good source for water. Agriculture is one of the main contributors to the economy.

Boise is the commercial center for much of the region. It is the home of a number of large corporations and is also the state capital. It also is the cultural and entertainment center for much of south Idaho.

Public education in southern Idaho is good. There are four fine institutions of higher learning that serve southern Idaho. Medical facilities are available in each of the communities. The smaller communities rely on the regional hospitals in the larger metropolitan areas for cases requiring specialized treatment.

Boise's and Salt Lake's airports are the main sources of national and international flights. Commuter flights are available from the medium size communities.

Boise (142,000 Pop.)

Boise is one of the largest communities in the Northwest to be visited. It is an attractive city located in what some call "Treasure Valley". It is the golden hues that catch one's eye and this is perhaps why it has the nickname. The southern beginnings of the Sawtooth Range mountains, immediately north of the city, are relatively bare and have a rolling appearance. The Boise River flows through the city and has enabled the folks of Boise to develop a 25 mile long green belt with trails along the river.

Downtown Boise is a pleasant place to visit with its combination of high rise buildings and older historic structures. Large trees shade the grounds of many of the state building and there are a number of small parks that make warm summer days even more pleasant. The Chamber of Commerce touts Boise as a place where one will find a "unique balance of big city sophistication and small town friendliness." The city has a vitality that sparkles. It strikes one as a young community with the elegance of the past. The greater Boise area has a population of 342,000 people.

Boise has become the headquarters for a number of major corporations like Boise Cascade, Morrison Knudsen, J.R. Simplot, Ore-Ida Foods, Micron Technology, Albertson's, TJ International, West One Bank, BMC West and Idaho Power. The economy rests primarily on agriculture, food processing, timber, high technology, government agencies and the supportive services. The economy is stable and unemployment is low. The cost of living is slightly higher than the national average. Utility costs are relatively low when compared to other communities on the East and West coasts.

Real estate costs are not prohibitive. A new three bedroom/two bath home in a nice neighborhood will range from $100,000 up to the mid $100,000s. A similar home with a view or on a golf course can be found from the mid $100,000s to the low $200,000. There are certainly nice homes that will run higher but not much over $350,000. Lots are relatively inexpensive. One thing a person notices is the abundance of homes that are ranch style (single story). This is not always the case in areas where land is more expensive.

Idaho

The police and fire departments are manned by well trained professionals. The fire personnel are trained to respond to all types of emergencies. 911 service is available and the response time averages about three minutes. The serious crime rate for Boise is below the national average.

There are two major medical centers plus a VA hospital, a psychiatric hospital and a rehabilitation center located in Boise. The hospitals are capable of providing a comprehensive health program and serve the people of southwestern Idaho and northeastern Oregon. St. Lukes Hospital was rated as one of the top 100 hospitals in the nation. The combined number of beds provided by these medical facilities amounts to over 800.

The public schools are modern, well maintained and present an environment that is conducive to learning. The students place well above the national average in many of the national tests. The staffs are well trained and over 60% of them have master's degrees or above.

There are three fine institutions of higher learning in the vicinity of Boise. Boise State University serves 15,000 students; the nationally recognized Albertson's College serves 700 students and is considered to be one of the best liberal arts college in the West; and Northwest Nazarene College provides a fine education for its 1,200 students. All three of these institutions are considered outstanding.

Boise has a first class airport that is served by seven commercial airlines. This is the center where nearly all southwestern Idaho and northeastern Oregon come for commercial flights in and out of the region.

The cultural climate in Boise is superb. The area supports a professional philharmonic orchestra, a dance group and an opera company. Two performing arts centers are available for local, national and international performances. On any given night one might be able to attend performances of Shakespeare, *The Nutcracker*, music of the great masters performed by an outstanding philharmonic orchestra or a famous operatic production.

There are several museums that attract attention. One rather unusual museum is a facility dedicated to the study and perpetuation of the Basques and their contribution to the West.

Idaho

One can find any number of events that are less "heavy" and perhaps more active. For example, Boise hosts the Nike Boise Open—a golf tournament, the Boise River Festival, the National Old Time Fiddlers Contest, the Idaho International Womens' Challenge—a bike race, and everyone's favorite: the Western Idaho Fair.

Recreation is focused on the outdoors as is the case in most of the Northwest. The mountains provide snow in the winter which makes snowmobiling and cross country skiing available. Downhill skiing is available at Bogus Basin only 16 miles away from the city. For those who want of do a bit of driving before skiing, there is the famous Sun Valley. In the summer these mountains provide areas for hiking, camping and rafting. Yellowstone National Park, the Grand Tetons and Craters of the Moon are within a reasonable distance.

The city provides all sorts of opportunities for recreation. The population is relatively young and they enjoy the more active activities such as football, softball, tennis, golf biking, basketball, soccer, skating, swimming and tubing on the Boise River.

Boise is located in southwestern Idaho not far from the Oregon line. Because of its location it has, over the years, become quite self sufficient. If one wants to go to another large metropolitan area, the drive is a "fer piece". Salt Lake City is the closest big city and it is 336 miles to the south. Spokane is 384 miles to the north, Seattle is 517 miles and Portland is 432 miles to the northwest. The airplane is a very popular vehicle for travel to and from Boise.

Summary: Boise is a vibrant community. Its climate is dry with warm summers and relatively mild winters. Recreational and cultural opportunities are abundant. The schools are good, health services are excellent, the cost of living is not too high, city services are good, and the economy is stable. This is a good place to raise children. The folks work hard and for the most part appear to be "God fearing". If a person is tired of life in a large urban area but not quite ready to give up some of the conveniences, then Boise is a good choice. Visit and see for yourself.

Idaho

Ketchum, Sun Valley and Elkhorn (3,500 Pop.)

This is an area that even the post cards do not do justice. It is absolutely gorgeous. The Wood River flows through this picturesque mountain valley. The evergreen forest provide a green carpet spotted with golden hillsides and meadows. The town of Ketchum, the main commercial area, is right out of a Warren Miller ski film about fabulous ski towns. Needless to say the area is tourist oriented. Ketchum provides many of the cultural and entertainment events for the surrounding community. Sun Valley and Elkhorn are destination resort communities. In the winter this area is focused on snow sports and in the summer hiking, horseback riding, golf, tennis, and rafting take over.

Real estate prices will test your pocket book! In perusing the real estate buyer's guides, the homes advertised ranged from $400,000 up to $2,000,000 plus. Condos are more reasonable with starting prices in the lower $200,000 and up. Be advised that if a person is serious about buying in this area then they better have a strong heart and plenty of money. It did seem that for such a small area that there were a very large number of homes for sale. One wonders what that says about the turnover.

If one wants to enjoy the fruits of living in such a beautiful area and doesn't care to invest such large amounts in housing, than a practical alternative is to go down the road to Hailey and Bellevue. Homes in this area a far more reasonable and a person is only 12 to 16 miles away from Ketchum. Folks say that the trend in housing prices in these communities are definitely on the rise.

Police protection is provide by a combination of services from the state police, county sheriff and city police staffs. Fire protection is a combination of paid staff and volunteers. The paid fire personnel are trained as emergency medical technicians. The entire county is linked with 911 services.

The valley has a complement of over 40 doctors - perhaps a reflection of their lifestyle preferences combined with professional service opportunities. The Wood River Medical Center has two locations, one in Hailey and one in Sun Valley. These facilities are capable of handling all but those cases

Idaho

that require the specialized services that are found in larger metropolitan centers.

The public schools in the area provide both academic and vocational programs. The enrollment is about 2,700. The students score well on national tests and over 75% attend higher education after graduation from high school.

The College of Southern Idaho offers classes leading to a GED and an Associates Degree. This institution also provides for noncredit classes in a variety of subjects.

The airport for this area is located in Hailey. The Friedman Memorial Airport has a 6,600 foot runway, a control tower, and service facilities. Horizon Air and Sky West fly in and out of Friedman. Boise and Salt Lake provide connections for national and international flights.

Culturally, the area benefits from having luxurious destination resorts. These resorts bring national and international talent to the area. These entertainers coupled with the local talent make for a wide variety of cultural experiences. A sample of the variety offered is shown by the following: Sun Valley Music Festival, Elkhorn Music Festival, Sun Valley Pro Musica, Sun Valley Repertory Company, Antique Fair, Jazz Jamboree, ice shows, and a Performing Arts Theater as well as over 20 fascinating art galleries.

When it comes to recreation, outdoor opportunities abound. There is downhill skiing during the winter on Baldy and Dollar mountains. Some of the best skiing that the world has to offer is found here and the facilities are first class. Where there is downhill skiing one knows that cross country skiing can not be far away. Of course, there is also snowmobiling, sleigh rides, ice skating, heli-skiing, and snowshoeing.

It comes as a surprise to most people that this area, noted for skiing, really has more visitors during the summer than in the winter months. This region with its mountains and Sawtooth National Recreational Area, has many exciting pursuits to follow during the warmer weather. The lakes and rivers provide opportunities for boating, swimming, river rafting, and fishing. The mountains allow mountain climbing, backpacking, camping, photography, and paragliding. The valley has a number of excellent golf courses, bike and hiking trails. Also popular are balloon rides, ice skating, tennis and swimming. This region is also noted for big game hunting opportunities.

Ketchum and the surrounding communities are not on the beaten path. It takes some effort to get there but once there, it is well worth it. Boise is 154 miles to the west and Salt Lake is 282 miles to the south.

Summary: A person should have considerable wealth if they are interested in buying a nice house in the Sun Valley area. Single family dwellings are expensive. On the other hand condos appeared to be much more reasonable. Hailey or Bellevue just down the road from Ketchum offer alternatives for housing. The cost of living in the area is high. The city services are certainly adequate. The medical center in Ketchum is capable of servicing most of the health problems encountered in the general population. The schools are good but local higher education opportunities appear to be limited. Certainly, the cultural and recreational opportunities are superior. The area is geographically isolated but with all that is available who would want to go anywhere. If one must travel, the air service is reasonable and the roads are good.

Why would one want to live in the Sun Valley area? There are several reasons. The outdoor recreational opportunities are about the best one will find in the United States. The cultural and entertainment environment is very rewarding. The scenic beauty is unsurpassed. In short, it is a very exciting and wholesome environment. It would make an excellent choice for a "snowbird" or an avid skier.

Stanley (71 Pop.)
(Yes, that's right - 71 people)

Stanley is really a different place. It reminds one of what an Alaskan settlement might be like. It is tucked in between two mountain ranges—the Sawtooth and the Lost River. The valley is blessed with the "River of No Return" better known as the Salmon River. The valley is a model for the typical National Geographic story about the rugged and pristine high mountain country in the great West. Stanley is at the

Idaho

merging point of three scenic by ways: the Sawtooth, the Salmon, and the Ponderosa Pine.

The economy is sustained by cattle ranches and tourism. The ranches host visitors who want to see what the West is really like and the river and mountains supply adventures for other visitors. The 71 folks who reside in Stanley are devoted to providing service to the ranchers and the visitors.

Real estate opportunities are in short supply. It is suggested if one is interested in finding a home, cabin, land or ranch, they should seek out a good Realtor. If while you are visiting and you come across a gentleman driving an International Scout that looks like a Holstein cow and has Texas longhorn horns on the front, stop and talk to him. He is a fascinating person and he happens to be the only Realtor in town. A nicer gentleman you won't meet.

The volunteer fire department is well trained in fire fighting and EMT services. The police services are provided by Custer County Sheriffs. Medical care is primarily devoted to emergencies and common health concerns. A certified registered nurse practitioner and an emergency medical technician staff the clinic. The Wood River Medical Center in Ketchum supports the clinic. Ambulance and Life Flight services are available.

A two room school house with two teachers is available for the children K-8. High school students are bussed 65 miles northeast to Challis.

Culturally, these folks are left to their own devices. The Sawtooth Mountains Mamas put on an annual arts and crafts fair and a person wouldn't want to miss the Sawtooth Quilt Festival. Lest a person think that this community is without culture there is the Concert and Cowboy Poetry function. Other highlights are the Gem and Mineral Show, the Fireman's Ball, Casino Night, and the annual Kite Flying Contest.

Recreationally this community looks to the river and the mountains. The adventures are much the same as are enjoyed throughout the Northwest. The Salmon River and its whitewater rafting trips are, perhaps, unique to this region. If it is the outdoors that a person likes, then this is the place.

The weather is different in this valley from those that have been previously discussed. The altitude of the valley is between 6,000 and 7,000 feet. The surrounding mountains rise to over 10,000 feet. The growing season is 20 days—not a place for an avid gardener. The summer days are pleasantly warm and the evenings cool. The winter is for the hearty. Temperatures can be as cold as any place in the United States. In fact, Stanley competes with International Falls, Minnesota, for lowest winter temperatures in the continental U.S. Snowmobiles and a four-wheel truck are good forms of winter transportation. In the spring and early summer, when the mountain snows melt, a ride down the Salmon River can be very, very exciting.

Summary: If one wants to get away from it all, then Stanley might just be the place. Life is simpler there and one learns that their neighbor can be counted on when the going gets tough. Life can be hard there but the beauty of the region and the freedom that one feels is rare in the continental United States. Remember, if you go to Stanley be sure to keep an eye open for a "four wheeled Holstein".

Salmon (3,000 Pop.)

In the eastern part of Idaho is the small community of Salmon. It is located in a valley that is considered high desert. It is surrounded by high mountains, sage brush, cottonwood trees, a national wilderness area of over 2 million acres and of course the beautiful Salmon River which flows smoothly through the community. This is a section of the nation that exhibits the "bigness" of this nation. Lemhi County, in which Salmon is located, is four times the size of Rhode Island. Salmon's population makes up 50% of the county's population.

Salmon's economy is primarily supported by agriculture. Government agencies, mining, manufacturing, retail trade and tourism add to the economy. Salmon serves as a regional center for retail, commercial enterprises and medical services. Energy cost and the cost of living is relatively low.

Real estate in Salmon and the surrounding area is reasonable when compared to some of the urban areas of the West. A newer three bedroom/two bath home will run from $120,000 to $150,000. Homes on small acreages will run from $130,000 to $200,000. A log home on 5 acres was listed for $175,000. River front land runs about $11,000 per acre. The Scenic River Corridor, to the north of Salmon, on the Salmon River is more expensive. This section of land presents a person with a pioneer environment—wild animals, no utilities, few people, a gorgeous river and unmatched scenery.

Salmon has a paid police force and is the home for the county sheriff and state patrol. The fire department is staffed by volunteers and, like most small communities, the volunteers do a fine job. There is a small hospital, Steele Memorial Hospital, with 35 beds. The hospital in Missoula, St. Pat's, supports the medical services of Salmon. Also, Eastern Idaho Regional Medical Center in Idaho Falls is available for support.

The community does not have 911 at the present time. Efforts are being made to install such a system sometime in the near future.

The public school district is small with an enrollment of about 1,300. The dropout rate is relatively low and approximately 57% of the graduates go on to college. The school system curriculum reflects the needs of the community with college prep and vocational-technical programs. Because of its isolation, most post high school education is received at one of the higher educational institutions in Idaho or Montana. If any university staff comes to the community for extension courses, it is usually through the auspices of Idaho State University.

Salmon has a cinema. An arts association brings the performing arts to the community. It has some nice galleries with the works of local artists. The more festive activities include a Balloon Festival, a rodeo, a county fair and the famous Salmon River Days.

Outdoor recreation abounds, with river rafting and fly fishing being very popular. The usual downhill and cross country skiing, snowmobiling, hiking, horseback riding, camping, "RVing", and hunting are all available.

The weather is fairly typical for high desert in a mountain valley. It snows in the winter but not as much as one would expect. Twenty-seven inches annually is pretty standard for the valley floor. Precipitation is about 9 inches during any given year. The low temperatures in the winters will average from 5 degrees to 20 degrees. Summers high temperatures will average between 80 and 90 degrees.

Salmon is probably one of the most isolated communities in the Northwest. Missoula is approximately 130 miles to the north and Idaho Falls is 162 miles to the south. A shopping trip can be a two day affair. The roads in winter weather can be very exciting.

Summary: If one wants to go to a community that enjoys the mystic of the "River of No Return", than Salmon is the place. It is small, friendly and has most of the services that one will need to live a simple life. The people are said to be somewhat independent in their nature, probably much like their forefathers. Real estate is reasonable and the cost of living is not out-of-line. If one has a critical medical condition one should think seriously about looking for a community where critical care medical services might be more readily available. Salmon is for the friendly, bold, strong and independent person.

Western Montana Map

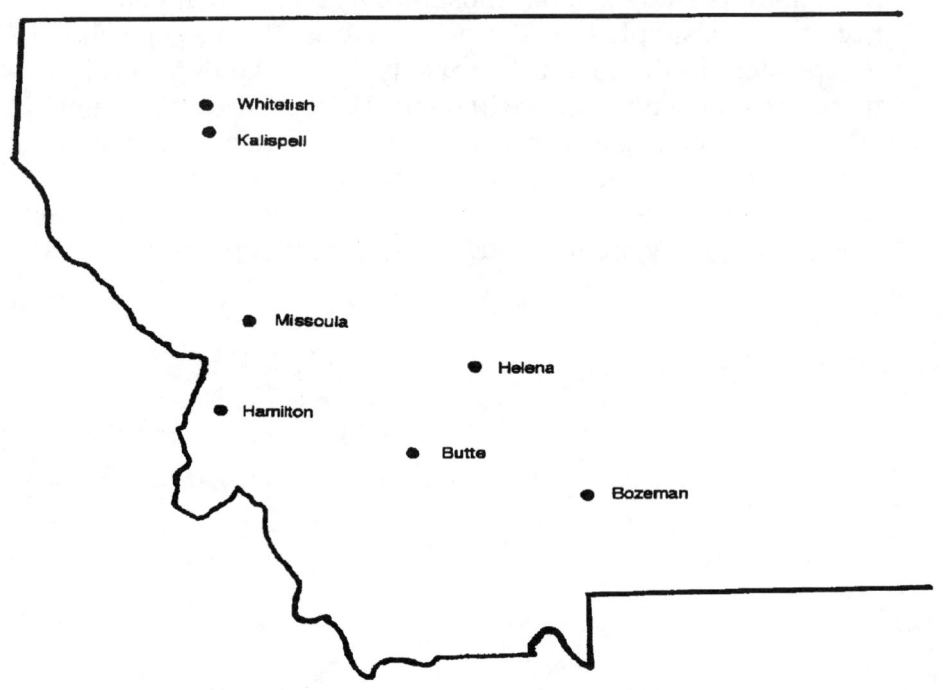

MONTANA (799,065 Pop.)

It is difficult to think of a better opening to describe Montana than that given by the governor, "In so many wondrous ways, Montana is what America used to be—148,000 square miles of vast plains, pure water, snowy peaks, sprawling forest, rich resources, a staggering array of wildlife ..." (Montana Official Highway Map 1995-1996) It is one of the most fascinating and beautiful places on this planet!

The western third of Montana is mountainous with beautiful valleys. The mountains provide the snow pack that feeds the crystal clear streams, rivers and lakes. Forests of ponderosa, fir, and larch cling to the mountain slopes while the valleys are dotted with neat farms and ranches.

Eastern Montana is part of the Great Plains, much like North Dakota and Wyoming. Here one finds miles of plains, rolling hills, cattle, wheat, historical monuments and Indian reservations. The summers are hot and the winters are cold and windy.

Montana is a vast area and the population for the whole state is not much larger then the populations of such cities as San Francisco, San Jose or Indianapolis. The state is the fourth largest state in the United States and is just a trifle bit larger than Germany or Japan. Montana is indeed a place where someone could go if they want real solitude. On the other hand, it has some wonderful cities and towns and a number of them will be described later in this presentation.

The economy of the state is supported mainly by agriculture, forestry products and mining. Almost two thirds of the land is given to farms and ranches. The average size of a farm or ranch is almost 2,500 acres. Wheat, hay and cattle are the mainstays of the agricultural community. Forests cover almost one-quarter of the state, mostly in the western third. The production of lumber and wood products is the states leading industry. Montana's mineral production is one of the highest in the United States. Petroleum, natural gas, coal, copper, gold and other lessor minerals are found there. Electricity production in Montana is one of the highest in the United States. Some high-tech industries are starting to appear in places like Butte and Kalispell and other larger communities. Tourism,

Western Montana

due to Montana's travel industry's efforts, is growing and becoming an important factor in the state's economy. Montana's taxes are the third lowest in the United States, beat only by Alaska and Delaware. (*Kiplinger's Personal Finance Magazine*, August 1995, pp.58-59)

Real estate prices are relatively inexpensive. In the smaller communities visited, a newer three bedroom/two bath home can be found around $100,000. In the larger cities visited that price went up by $20,000 to $50,000 for a similar home.

When it comes to education, the state does a creditable job. 94.5 percent of its high school pupils graduate. That is 6th highest in the nation. There are five post- secondary vocational and technical school located in the larger communities of the state. There are six state institutions of higher learning and three private colleges.

Also there are three state funded community colleges. The Native American tribal councils offer post secondary education at community colleges located on their reservations.

Culturally, Montana has a rich pioneer and Native American heritage. There are seven Indian reservations in Montana. Tribal names, such as Cheyenne, Blackfeet, Sioux, Chippewa and Crow, stir the imagination of those who dream of days past with their simpler and more natural ways. There are a large number of museums in the state and libraries are also numerous. The institutions of higher learning are also responsible for providing many cultural and entertainment opportunities. The larger cities usually have such activities as amateur theater, symphony, ballet, opera, and performances by national and international entertainers. The smaller communities and, for that matter the larger cities, have many interesting rodeos and festivals.

Recreationally, Montana has abundant opportunities. Downhill skiing is some of the best in the nation. Of course, where downhill is available so then is cross country skiing, snowmobiling, and ice fishing. The mountains and rivers provide for hiking, camping, hunting, fishing, climbing and soaring. If ones taste run to the outdoors, then Montana is the place.

Montana is a large area. It is over 500 miles west to east and 320 miles north to south. Three major highways cross

Western Montana

the state. I-90 and I-94 are the major west and east routes. A lesser highway, U.S. 2, in the northern part of the state transverses the state from west to east, I-15 runs north and south. The major cities have commercial air service. The Burlington Northern provides rail services.

During the winter, a minus on the thermometer is a familiar sight to the folks in Montana. The summer months can be warm to just plain hot depending on the location. The summers and winters in western Montana can be less severe than is the case for eastern Montana. The folks in Montana have to be a hardy breed. Western Montana has a great deal of appeal for those who are fascinated by high mountains, gorgeous silvery streams, big lakes, wildlife, a simpler lifestyle and friendly people.

For purposes of this presentation the discussion will focus only on the western third of the state. This is the part of Montana that blends with the Pacific Northwest theme.

Kalispell (11,900 Pop.)

The Flathead Valley is a place one would swear they had seen in movies about Indians and mountain men. It is absolutely one of the most gorgeous places on the face of the earth. Mountains ring the valley, crystal clear rivers and lakes abound, orderly farms and orchards dot the landscape and wildlife is plentiful.

This magnificent valley covers about 5,100 square miles, which is larger than several of the New England states. The Flathead Lake, 27 miles long, 6 -15 miles wide and with a shoreline measuring 124 miles, is the largest fresh water lake west of the Mississippi.

To the north of the valley is Glacier National Park with over a million acres within its boundaries. There are 48 glaciers, 200 lakes and 700 miles of trails within the Park's borders.

Kalispell is an important part of this region. It is the largest city and provides for the bulk of commercial activity. Wood products, agriculture and tourism provide the economic base for the region. The regional medical facilities of Kalispell and light industry supplement this base. The mountain forests supply the timber which is processed in Kalispell and the smaller communities of the Valley. Agriculture contributes to the economy through the production of grains, fruits, Christmas trees, mint and seed potatoes. Tourism, another important aspect of the economy, is benefited by the closeness of Flathead Lake, Glacier National Park, Big Mountain Ski Resort and the general beauty of the area. These features bring hundreds of thousands of visitors to Kalispell and the valley every year.

Local leaders are very active in seeking light industry to broaden the area's economic base. One of the advantages of locating a business in the greater Kalispell area is the sophistication of the work force and the relatively low cost of labor. As with many communities now days, any industry that does come to the area must be compatible with the community's concerns for the health of its people and its natural environment. In addition to the private economic contributors in the Kalispell area, there are many local, state and federal agencies that employ large numbers of the residents.

There are some very nice older homes in Kalispell and a number of new home developments on the city's outskirts. In some of the older sections of town a visitor will find "Rockwellian" scenes where the streets are shaded by stately old trees, the lawns are manicured and large wood framed homes with comfortable front porches just made for that favorite easy chair and a refreshing glass of lemonade exist. If one did not know better, they might think they were in a quaint Midwestern or Eastern village.

The developments on the outskirts of town are familiar sites to the urbanite. The typical development is exemplified by three or four bedroom wood frame homes with young trees, neat lawns and wide blacktopped streets.

The cost of housing, according to real estate multiple listing figures, has doubled between 1987 and 1994. The cost to an outsider still looks very reasonable but, with the low wages paid in the valley, the cost is beyond the means of many of the local residents. The average cost started to level out in 1993 and price increases have continued to rise only slightly in the mid 1990s.

Western Montana

A new three bedroom/two bath home will start in the high $90,000s. Homes with small acreage will start at about $140,000 and go up. A golf course home can be found in the high $100,000s. River acreage on the Flathead River, with a home, will be in the mid $200,000s. Lake views of the Flathead Lake will vary considerably in price depending on the location. There are some substantial view homes that will sell in the low $200,000. Smaller lakes in the area can have homes and sites that are less expensive.

One of the features that the people of Kalispell are especially proud of is the Kalispell Regional Hospital. This is a modern, 110 bed facility that can provide comprehensive services to its patients. The philosophy of the hospital is exemplified in its visionary Wellness and Fitness Program. "Pill hill", where the hospital is located along with numerous supportive clinics, gives the community a fine medical center complex.

In addition to the health services of the medical center, a person will find a modern 911 system, a quick response and disaster preparedness service, plus an ALERT helicopter service. The police and fire services are modern and first rate.

A county public school system serves Kalispell. The enrollment for the system is 13,000, which makes for an efficient size. The district can afford a modern and comprehensive program for the youth of the community and it is recognized for high academic standards and a low dropout rate.

Flathead Valley Community College has an enrollment of approximately 1,800 and provides a broad academic and vocational-technical program that fits the community's needs. The University of Montana, at Missoula, provides extension courses for those interested in pursuing an advanced degree or improving their skill or knowledge level.

The community is served by two airports. Eight miles to the northeast of Kalispell is the modern Glacier International Airport with its 8,000 foot runway. Kalispell has a smaller facility serving charter and private aircraft.

The summers are pleasant and the falls are beautiful. The winters are cold and snow is a frequent visitor.

Western Montana

Kalispell is large enough to support many of the cultural activities that can add so much to a person's life. The city is earning the reputation in Montana as one of the better art centers. Kalispell has a western tradition and there are a number of museum and art galleries that focus on that theme. The city has a number of theater, orchestra and choral groups. It is not unusual for folks in Kalispell to go to Big Fork for theater or Whitefish for a festival. To the Westerner, traveling 200 miles to see a good football game or a New York stage production that is "in town" is no "big deal".

As for outdoor recreational opportunities, there are a myriad of activities in which one can engage. There is downhill skiing, snowmobiling, cross country skiing at Big Mountain and the surrounding hills. The lakes provide opportunities for fishing, boating, water skiing and wind surfing. The rivers provide great sport fishing and rafting. Golf is available at the Buffalo Hill Golf Course located in the northern part of Kalispell, and there are a number of other courses in nearby Columbia Falls, Big Fork and White Fish.

Animal watching and hunting are popular and the rewards are sometimes beyond what one expects. The National Bison Range is a unique experience for a person interested in seeing the big shaggy beast up close. In addition to the bison, one can catch a glimpse of elk, deer, and antelope on the Range.

Kalispell is somewhat isolated but that is not a major concern. It is large enough to have, about everything a person could want. If a person does want to go the "big city" Spokane is 225 miles to the west. Missoula is 125 miles to the southeast and Calgary, Canada is about 225 miles to the north.

Summary: Kalispell is a vigorous city located in a beautiful valley. It has good civic services and is large enough to provide good shopping and housing opportunities. The schools are good, medical services are modern and comprehensive and cultural activities abound. The Valley affords a variety of outdoor recreational opportunities. Kalispell does not have a great many job opportunities and the wages are relatively low. It is the beauty of the area and the vitality of the of the people that will draw a person to Kalispell.

Western Montana

Whitefish (4,400 Pop.)

About 14 miles north of Kalispell, one comes upon the little town of Whitefish which is on, what else, Whitefish Lake. This town is at the foot of Big Mountain, the home of the Big Mountain Ski Resort. This is a Western town that has become quite popular with several entertainment celebrities. There are a large number of retirees in the town and the surrounding country side.

The economy of Whitefish is tied to the economy of the Flathead Valley. People in Whitefish will work in Kalispell, Columbia Falls and Big Mountain. As with the rest of the valley, jobs are not plentiful. Tourism, "railroading", wood products and agriculture play major roles in the economy.

One of the chief characteristics of the Whitefish real estate market is that new construction is in short supply. The inventory in Whitefish is limited. A new three bedroom/two bath home will run in the low $100,000s. There are some older homes available at prices less than new construction. Many of these need remodeling or, at least, TLC. With a relatively small investment many of the older homes can be made quite presentable. Homes on small acreages are available in the mid $100,000s.

Big Mountain Resort residences are also available. A three bedroom/two bath townhouse at Big Mountain can be purchased in the high $100,000s Homes on Whitefish Lake run in the neighborhood of $400 - $600 thousand. Waterfront land will cost $2,500 to $3,000 per linear foot.

Whitefish has a 44 bed hospital. The Kalispell Regional Hospital provides service for the patients who need special treatment. 911 service is available. The police department is manned by 12 full-time officers and the fire department depends on volunteers.

The public school system has an enrollment at just over 2,000 pupils. According to information furnished by the school district, the Whitefish students average score on state tests are above the state average. On college entrance exams, the average of Whitefish students is higher than scores of fellow students at the state and national levels.

Western Montana

The Flathead Valley Community College provides a good two-year academic and vocational-technical program. The University of Montana provides extension classes for those interested in pursuing a four-year degree or increasing their skill and knowledge level.

Whitefish's contribution to the culture of the valley is the Whitefish Theatre Company. In addition to its performances, the Company also sponsors a summer camp for young people. Big Mountain sponsors musical and ballet workshops. During the month of July, Whitefish participates in the valley's Flathead Festival.

Other communities also contribute to Whitefish's cultural environment, through such programs as a children's choir, community orchestras and string quartets and a variety of artist pursuits. Another interesting feature available to the citizen of Whitefish is the valley's Flathead Quilters Guild. Sounds like a great place to gather on a cold day for a cup of coffee, some good conversation and creative expression.

The town has a very strong and well funded historical society. This society owns the old Northern Pacific Railroad Depot which houses the museum, the Chamber of Commerce and several businesses.

As for outdoor activities, there is boating, fishing, hunting, downhill skiing, snowmobiling, cross country skiing, hiking, rafting and on and on. You name it and the valley and Whitefish will probably have it.

Whitefish is 58 miles from the Canadian border. Spokane is a five hour drive and Missoula is about three hours away. Kalispell is 20 minutes to the south and the drive to Big Fork will take the better part of an hour.

Summary: Whitefish does not have a lot of housing inventory. There are some very expensive homes available. Country homes outside of Whitefish are probably more available than homes in Whitefish. Jobs are scarce and competition is fierce. There are plenty of "ski" folks who are looking for work so they can stay in Whitefish. Most of the jobs are located in other communities.

For a small community, the town has adequate protection services. The medical center at Kalispell is a plus when coupled with the facilities in Whitefish. Culturally and entertainment-wise, one will come to rely upon the Valley for a number of opportunities.

Taking all this into consideration, Whitefish is still a desirable place to live if one doesn't have to depend heavily upon the community for making a living. This is a skiers paradise and many folks love the outdoor focus of the area. Don't forget the winters can be long, gray and cold but the skiing and the folks are great!

Missoula (42,900 Pop.)

Missoula is the first major Montana city a person comes to when traveling east from Idaho on Interstate 90. It is often referred to as the "City of Five Valleys". The city is nestled among the Bitterroot, Sapphire and Garnet mountain ranges with the beautiful Clark Fork River cutting through the city. All of this gives a renovated downtown a very picturesque environment.

The valley slopes upward toward the heavily forested mountains, providing many splendid view sites for houses. The city proper is well organized with tree lined boulevards that remind a person of a town one might find in the East. The homes in the older sections of town are well maintained. The homes on the outskirts of the city are more contemporary and it is here that one finds some small acreage plots. The city serves as a regional center for much of western Montana. One gets the distinct impression that this is a city in which people strive hard to keep it a pleasant place to live.

The economy of the city is primarily supported by the wood and paper industry, motor carrier companies, federal agencies, tourism, and the University of Montana. The fact that it is a regional trade center is also very important to the economic well-being of the community. The cost of living is slightly above the national average but significantly below the larger urban areas in the West. The unemployment rate usually runs around 5%.

Western Montana

Housing is more expensive than one will find in other parts of the state, but it is reasonably priced by coastal and urban standards. To the south of Missoula are properties that are less expensive and within a comfortable commuting distance. In the Missoula area a newer three bedroom/two bath home can be found in the mid $100,000. Many of the homes have basements. Basements are not unusual for the Midwest or the East but are not a characteristic of much of the West. When looking at a home in Montana, always remember that it can get quite cold there and that good insulation and heating is essential.

Missoula is a modern city and its services reflect this. The police and fire protection services are manned by well trained full-time professionals. The schools are first class. The enrollment is about 9,700 which allows for a broad curriculum. The teacher/pupil ratio is low.

The University of Montana has a beautiful campus near the downtown of Missoula. This University has turned out it share of scholars, with Rhodes Scholars accounting for 25 while International Fulbright Scholars number 31.

There are two hospitals in Missoula with a total of 336 beds. St. Pat's is the regional hospital and it delivers a comprehensive program of services including cancer treatment and coronary surgery. The Community Medical Center also provides a comprehensive program but focuses more in the area of rehabilitation and Ob/Gyn services.

This area has four seasons with nice summers and cold winters. Occasionally a freezing fog or snow makes winter driving difficult.

Missoula is located on Interstate 90 which is a major east-west highway crossing the nation. The community also has good rail services. Commercial air services are provided by Delta, Northwest and Horizon.

When it comes to culture, Missoula provides a wide variety of opportunities. The community has live theater, string and chamber groups, symphony, and a variety of museums and galleries. A unique feature of the cultural environment in the Missoula area is its nationally acclaimed Children's Theater. This theater produces a number of splendid performances in the community and elsewhere throughout the nation. It is

Western Montana

estimated that over 15,000 children in 200 communities participate in this program.

Another outstanding feature is the Carousel for Missoula. This is the first hand carved carousel built anywhere since the Great Depression in the 30's. Volunteers put in 100,000 hours carving, sanding, and painting to bring this dream to fruition. It was a community effort that typifies the spirit of the people of Missoula. The Carousel is located beside the Clark Fork River at One Caras Park in downtown Missoula.

As is the case with many western towns, Missoula is quite self sufficient. But if a person does have to go some place, they will find Spokane 207 miles to the west with Seattle being a long 488 miles in the same direction. To the south, Salt Lake is 500 miles and Butte, to the east, is 120 miles.

Summary: Missoula is a very pleasant city. It has many cultural and recreational opportunities. The University is a big positive to the community as are the medical services. Housing is slightly higher than some other communities in the Northwest but still very reasonable when compared to the coast and larger urban areas. The downtown is alive and the economy is diversified. All in all, Missoula has great appeal and provides a wholesome environment.

Hamilton (3,100 Pop.)

Hamilton is a small town in the Bitterroot Valley approximately 40 miles south of Missoula. The valley is broad and between two mountain ranges with the rugged Bitterroots on the west and the less rugged Sapphire Range on the east. The valley floor is relatively flat with gentle slopes up each side as the valley works it way into the mountains. This region is primarily dedicated to agricultural and livestock. Irrigation is evidenced on many of the farms and ranches. Cottonwood and pine are found scattered throughout the valley and especially along the banks of the Bitterroot, a river which meanders its way through the valley.

Hamilton, a town of 3,100 inhabitants, is fairly typical of a Western town. It has its older sections, which for the most

Western Montana

part have been reasonably maintained. There is evidence of some remodeling and refurbishing going on. The streets are broad, tree lined and sprinkled with some grand old homes. The outer limits of the town are showing ample evidence of newer contemporary development. The ranch-type homes are numerous which indicates that land is less expensive than in the more urban areas of the West. Also, ranch homes (ramblers) are popular with the senior citizens. The downtown has broad streets and neat shops and businesses. Highway 93 runs through the commercial part of town. Hamilton is the county seat of Ravalli County, the fastest growing county in Montana.

The economy of Hamilton is dependent upon agriculture, the log home industry, and it is the retail and commercial center of the region. The log home industry in nearby Stevensville, is a unique feature of the region's economy. The logs are fitted and marked as houses are assembled on the company's site, then disassembled and shipped to the buyer's site where they are reassembled. The work is seasonal, with only small crews working during the winter months. Another source of income to the economy is the large senior citizen population and tourism.

Housing is not particularly expensive when compared to many of the urban areas. A newer three bedroom/two bath home can be found in the low $100,000s. River frontage is in great demand. The river has a large flood plain where homes can not be built. Having to buy additional land to obtain river frontage and keep the building site above the flood plain, makes such home site expensive.

Land to the east of town, in the sage brush, can be much less expensive but water availability can be a problem. Some of the newer development to the southeast of town have homes that are quite reasonable and very good looking. Of course, there are older homes in the more established part of town that can be refurbished and provide one with a fine residence. Unlike many small communities, Hamilton has some nice looking town homes that sell from $125,000 to $138,000. Five acre ranchette type homes on the slopes to the west and east of town will start at about $140,000. There are a number of larger homes on acreage that are very attractive and can be purchased in the mid $200,000 range.

Hamilton has a paid police force and a low crime rate. The county sheriff's department is located in Hamilton. The fire department is composed of volunteers. 911 service is available. The Marcus Daly Hospital, a 48 bed facility, provides medical services to the region with backup for the most critical cases coming from St. Pat's Hospital in Missoula. Electricity is inexpensive and the community has natural gas.

Hamilton's airport has a 4,200 foot lighted landing strip. It services charters and private aircraft. Missoula, 46 miles away, provides for commercial and freight air service.

Each of the nearby towns has its own school system. Hamilton public schools have an enrollment of over 1,500 pupils. The University of Montana at Missoula provides for post high school education.

Culturally, the Hamilton area has community theater, museums, art galleries, rodeos, concerts and a number of traditional festivals. Missoula also provides a number of cultural and recreational opportunities for the folks in Hamilton.

Outdoor recreation is available on a grand scale in such a beautiful area. In the winter there is downhill skiing, cross-country skiing, snowmobiling and snowshoeing. The spring, summer and fall bring fishing, hunting, backpacking, hiking, horseback riding, camping, floating the river, wildlife watching and golf.

There are a number of "outfitters" who specialize in trips into the Bitterroots and guiding visitors to the trout streams that produce the "big ones." Fly fishing is big in this area. Just outside of nearby Darby, a sign giving credence to the importance of fishing reads: "Fishing is not a matter of life and death, it is more important than that."

The weather in the valley is probably as agreeable as one will find in Montana. Hamilton is called the "Banana Belt of Montana." The summers are quite comfortable and the winters have temperatures with highs in the 30s and 40s and lows in the 10s and 20s and sometimes considerably lower. The rain amounts to 12 to 15 inches annually. Snow on the valley floor is not a serious problem most of the time.

Western Montana

Summary: Hamilton is a fast growing area with a vital economy. It provides the retail, commercial and medical services for the area around the town. The services are adequate for a community of its size. The cost of living is low and real estate is relatively inexpensive. Certainly, recreation is abundant and cultural and entertainment activities are strengthened by Hamilton's closeness to the Missoula area. One thing to remember is this is a community that is growing fast and consequently it is and will be faced with some serious decisions regarding infrastructure and living styles. This challenge is not unique to Hamilton. Many small communities going through the "discover" phase are confronted with similar decisions. The folks of Hamilton are certainly capable of finding the right solutions and moving on. This is a nice place and is becoming quite popular.

Butte (33,400 Pop.)
(Including Silver Bow County)

History is very important to the Montana people. Butte is a good example of the effort people can go to preserve a piece of the past. When entering Butte one is struck by the old and the new. On the north side of Interstate 90 is the "old" part of town. This is where the history of the area is preserved. There are numerous old brick structure that are vivid reminders of the past glory days of Butte. This is where the Copper Kings built their luxurious mansions and business houses. The old buildings are, for the most part, in good repair and functional. Many of the banks, business offices and government quarters are located in this section of the town. Not only will one find evidence of past financial and business activity in this section of town but also many of the residences of the past are still evident and occupied. Architecturally, the structures represent the late 19th and early 20th century. Many have been renovated and actually are quite nice looking. This section of town is home to the main campus of Montana College of Science and Technology, an institution famous for its program dealing with mining.

On the south side of Interstate 90, one will find the newer section of Butte. This area houses the tourist facilities,

Western Montana

small business, industrial parks, high-tech industry and the airport. Farther south are nice residential areas, small acreages, and some view homes.

Butte is a town with lots of determination. In 1983 Anaconda, a giant copper mining company, started to phase out its huge open pit copper mining operation. Up to that time Anaconda and Butte were synonymous. Butte was a "company town" and without the company it was in for a rough time. The citizens of Butte rolled up their sleeves and set out to solve their problem. Part of the mining operation was purchased and reopened. Knowing the hazard of depending on one company for its economic well being the community sought to diversify. They have been quite successful in bringing in new industry and business enterprises.

About this time, the statute called "Our Lady of the Rockies" was placed on a 8,500 foot peak overlooking the city of Butte. The statue stands 90 feet tall and is stark white. It is a tribute to all the women of the West. Some attribute Butte's economic turn around to the presence of the statue.

The economy of Butte today is less dependent on mining than in years past. Mining is still important to the economy but other enterprises are filling in the void left by Anaconda. There are many mining and natural resource oriented companies located in Butte. ARCO's superfund cleanup facilities and a number of other high-tech enterprises call Butte home. Butte is the headquarters of the large energy concern called Montana Power. The economic scene, due to some hard work by the folks of Butte, has turned around from what it was in the mid 1980s.

Real estate comes in two packages. Up on the hill in the north part of town one can find older homes in the $30,000 to $50,000 range. Many of these homes are being purchased, renovated and rented. It is an area that reflects the days of yesteryear found so attractive by many folks. In this section of Butte there are also a number of homes that are in the normal price range for housing.

In the newer part of town, one can find a newer three bedroom/two bath home for $130,000 and up. Small acreages with a fairly new home can be found for $135,000 and up.

Western Montana

Larger homes with multiple acreage can be found at $200,000 and up. Land in comparison with West coast standards is not expensive. Generally speaking, real estate values are quite reasonable throughout the Butte area.

Butte and Silver Bow County operate as a consolidated city/county government. The police and fire departments operate with paid staff. The fire department has some volunteers also. Butte has 911. The St. James Hospital has 180 beds and provides a comprehensive program of medical services. Rivendell Psychiatric Center serves emotionally disturbed youths from the ages of 5 to 18.

The public school system provides a well rounded program. It has an enrollment of 5,600 plus pupils. Post high school educational opportunities are provided by Western Montana College, University of Montana and Montana College of Science and Technology.

The energy costs are low but the cold winters can require a lot of energy use. Butte has a modern airport with a 9,000 foot lighted runway. It provides service for charter, private and commercial aircraft.

Culturally, Butte has a lot to offer. It has a modern civic center capable of seating 3,500 to 6,000. This center provides for figure skating, hockey, basketball, wrestling, musical concerts, and trade fairs. Butte has a center for the performing arts as well as the recently restored, 72 year old, Fox Theater. The community supports a symphony, community concerts, Shakespeare in the Park, a number of amateur theater groups, numerous art galleries and many museums. Butte, like many other communities, has its annual festivals celebrating historical events and community holidays.

Outdoor activities cover the usual activities found in any community close to mountains and rivers. Butte has downhill skiing, snowmobiling, cross county skiing, ice fishing, backpacking, camping, boating, hunting, horseback riding, golf, rafting, and rock climbing. An activity not so common to other areas is speed skating. Butte is home to the U.S. High Altitude Sport Center. This is where many of the speed skaters come to train. Butte and the surrounding area also enjoy dog sled contests.

Western Montana

The weather in Butte can be very cold. The community is located in the mountains at a height of 5,000 plus feet. Temperatures can get down in the minuses and winter lasts from late October through March. The summers are warm and pleasant.

Summary: Butte has two faces. One is old but has a beauty that comes with things from the past. The "Pit" is just plain ugly. It is a cause for some environmental concerns that are being attended by the state and federal government. If one were to only focus on the "Pit," then Butte is not a place where one would be happy.

There is a lot more to Butte than that ugly mining scar. The people are a hearty bunch, friendly and looking to the future. There is a welcome mat out for new business and industry. The cultural and outdoor activities are abundant. Real estate is very reasonable. One additional caution, the winters are cold and fairly long. If cold weather is not your bag than perhaps Butte is not for you.

Bozeman (23,000 Pop.)

The thing that surprises a person when they come upon Bozeman is the openness of the land. Bozeman is in a large valley surrounded by several mountain ranges. The height of the distant mountains is in the 10,000 to 11,000 foot range. The valley is quite broad, thus the open feeling one gets.

Bozeman's growth has been slow but constant. The main economic drivers are agriculture, the University, government agencies and tourism—the west entrance to Yellowstone is only 90 miles to the south.

It is the regional commercial and retail center. The city gives considerable evidence of vitality and the economy appears to be stable and healthy. Bozeman is an attractive, and clean city. Many of the streets in the older section of town are broad and lined with giant old trees and neat homes.

Real estate is relatively inexpensive. A newer three bedroom/two bath home on a city lot will range $120,000 and up. Large contemporary homes on the outskirts of the city can be purchased in the mid $200,000 range. Homes on small acre-

Western Montana

ages near town, with view and fenced, can be purchased in the high $100,000 range. If one wants to go into ranching, there are some wonderful opportunities in the upper hundred of thousands of dollars range.

The police and fire departments are modern, efficient and both operate with paid staffs. Enrollment in the K-12 public system is about 5,000 pupils, which makes for an efficient district size. In the central part of the city a number of schools are located in a complex in conjunction with a large park and numerous athletic fields. Montana State University, a medium size university (10,900) is located in Bozeman. It is a school of modern facilities and a pleasant campus.

Bozeman has an airfield called Gallatin Field. It handles commercial as well a private and charter aircraft. Airlines serving Bozeman include Delta, Northwestern, and Horizon Air.

Deaconess Hospital serves the region. It is an 86 bed facility with comprehensive health services available. Bozeman has 911 service.

Bozeman has a symphony, an opera company, a theater company and ballet. In addition to the above cultural opportunities, one will find a number of museums and art galleries. One outstanding example of museums is the Museum of the Rockies, which presents the history of Montana from the age of the dinosaurs to the lifestyle of the 30s and 40s. Also, located in the city is the American Computer Museum which traces computation technology from the Egyptians to Windows 95. In the arts, the Emerson Cultural Center comes to the forefront with its galleries, displays and the performing arts programs.

Other events that reflect the lifestyles and interests of the community are the College National Finals Rodeo, the community rodeo, the Sweet Pea Festival, the Montana Winter Fair and the Gallatin County Fair.

As for recreation, well you name it and Bozeman can probably supply it. The famous Big Sky ski area is 40 miles to the south. This area gets 400 inches of snow each year and skiing is superb. It is a first class resort with town homes, condos and single family homes. The prices are not inexpensive but they are reasonable considering the desirableness of the area. Besides winter activities, Big Sky has summer activities which include golfing, hiking, fishing, and horseback riding.

To the north of Bozeman one finds another good ski area, not the size of Big Sky but very convenient. Bridger Bowl gets 350 inches of snow and provides groomed runs. It is less than 20 miles from the city. It also has housing facilities. As with the rest of Montana, snowmobiling and cross country skiing is also readily available. Rafting down the Gallatin River is a popular activity and, of course, hunting is big. If golf is one's game, there are at least 5 courses in or near Bozeman.

Bozeman has four seasons. In the summers the temperatures get into the 80s and 90s during the day with the evening being cool. The winters are cold but not record setting. Snow is plentiful during the winter. The valley is relatively flat so driving is not the challenge that one finds in mountain driving.

Bozeman is a self sufficient community but, by western standards, it is close to some larger communities which allows it to share in some of their opportunities. Billings is 168 miles to the east on I-90. Butte is 82 miles to the west and farther west is Missoula, 202 miles away.

Summary: Bozeman is a delightful community. The economy is stable and the services are more than adequate. Real estate prices are reasonable. The University is a big plus and the cultural and entertainment opportunities are plentiful. If one likes to ski, fish or hunt this is the spot. If one is looking for a ranch there are a number of opportunities nearby. There was something wholesome about Bozeman. (For some strange reason I came away from the valley with the feeling of calm exhilaration. It might have been the sun, the feeling of openness, or the simple beauty of the area, but what ever it was I look forward to another visit.)

Western Montana

Helena (24,600 Pop.)

The city is located at the foot of the Rocky Mountains and is only a short distant from the Continental Divide. The Rocky Mountains to the west rise to the height of 6,000 to 7,000 feet. Across a broad valley, to the east, is the Big Belt Range, with peaks in the 9,000 foot range. The Missouri River has it start about 50 miles to the south and it flows north, where it is intercepted by three dams in the valley just east of Helena. These dams form large beautiful lakes that give the people of Helena and the surrounding area a wonderful water playground.

Helena is the state capitol of Montana. It has some beautiful 19th century architecture that reflect the affluence of the gold mining frenzy of the late 1800s. Still a part of the community is Last Chance Gulch. The Gulch became the last chance for four miners before they were going to quit. It paid off and their success led to the gold rush that made Helena.

A portion of the city dates back to those wild and ostentatious times. The downtown is impressive with many brick building still in use that date back to the late 1800's and early 1900s. The streets are wide and flanked by beautiful old homes. Of course there are less pretentious homes scattered throughout the city. The downtown business section is clean and orderly. There are some rather unique structures in town. One is the Civic Center which has the appearance of a mosque. It was originally a Shriner's building. The Cathedral of Helena is beautiful and reflects the generosity of the very rich past.

The economy of the area is stable. A large number of the residents are employed by governmental agencies. Since Helena is the capitol, the state government is one of the largest employers. The Federal government also has many employees in the area and the public schools, as in most communities, is one of the larger employers. The hospital and a large medical insurance company provide over 1000 jobs. Service businesses are the next largest employers. Mining, agriculture and forestry round out the primary employment sources in the community. The unemployment rate is steady at about 5%, year in and year out.

Western Montana

A new three bedroom/two bath home will range from $120,000 to $150,000. View homes are pricey and property on the lake is generally higher than view property. It appears that very fine housing, some with view or water front, can be found in the area ranging from $150,000 up to $250,000. The prices seemed to be reasonable when compared to the West coast. New residential home construction has been on the increase in recent years. Housing costs are on the rise - no big surprise. Property taxes are relatively low - $1,300 for a $100,000 home. The cost of living is slightly lower than the national average. Most of the growth is coming from three states, California, Oregon and Washington.

Helena provides good police and fire protection. The outskirts rely on the county for police and fire protection. The public schools are first class. The students score well on national and state tests and approximately 60% of the graduates seek some form of higher education. Montana Vocational/Technical College is located in the community. This institution provides a 2-year program. Carroll College is also located in Helena and is a 4-year Catholic institution.

There are two hospitals providing a total of 220 beds. St. Peter's Hospital is the largest and provides comprehensive health care. Shadair Hospital focuses on the needs of children. There is also a Veteran Hospital in the community.

Helena Regional Airport is served by Delta and Horizon Air. The community is located on Interstate 15, a main north-south federal highway.

In the 1990 publication called *Life in America's Small Cities*, Helena was highly ranked for it diversion, education and sophistication This is as true today as it was in 1990.

Carroll College Theater and the Grand Street Theater provide excellent theater. The Community Concerts Association brings live performance to town during the year and Helena Present is responsible for bringing international and national performers, films, and workshops to the community. Helena has a symphony and chorale group. In the two and three dimensional arts, there is the Holter Museum of Art and the Montana Art Council. The Lewis and Clark Historical Society is located in Helena. Probably somewhat unique to

Western Montana

Helena is the Archie Bray Foundation which provides a residential center for potters.

Recreation is much the same as with other Montana regions. Unique to this area is the lake system formed by the dams on the Missouri River. This provides great boating, fishing, water skiing and even ice fishing opportunities.

As with the rest of Montana, Helena has nice summers and falls. The winters are cold and long. Helena is located 64 miles from Butte to the south and 115 miles from Missoula to the west. Spokane is 310 miles to the west, Seattle is 595 miles away and Salt Lake is 474 miles to the south. Cities in Montana are fairly well removed from the larger urban areas. This is one reason that cities in Montana are so self sufficient.

Summary: Helena has a rich cultural menu and is a mecca for recreational opportunities. Real estate is reasonable and the economy is stable. Services are adequate and the schools and educational opportunities are good. Helena has a fascinating historical background, especially for someone who is interested in the "old West." Many people who live there came to the community via a government job and when it came time to retire they stayed—that should tell us something. Helena gets considerable snow but with the right attitude that can be a source of great fun. Ice fishing, snowmobiling, cross country skiing and great downhill skiing are good examples of fun cold weather activities. Helena is certainly worth a visit.

Canada

British Columbia Map

BRITISH COLUMBIA (Pop. 3,500,000)

British Columbia has spectacular natural beauty. The province is bordered on the north by the Yukon Territory and Alaska, and to the south is Washington, Idaho and western Montana. It's neighbor to the east is Alberta and on the west is the Pacific, several straits, and numerous islands. British Columbia is larger than 49 of the United States states and it is the third largest province of Canada. Victoria, on Vancouver Island is the provincial capital.

It's Scandinavian-like seacoast is dotted with lovely fiords which are flanked with impressive snow-capped peaks. Thousands of islands dot the waters along the western seacoast and one island, Vancouver Island, is larger than several of the smaller New England states.

Mountains play home to vast forests, raging rivers, gigantic glaciers, huge lakes and hundreds of smaller sister lakes. The dominant mountain ranges are the Coast Mountains, in the west; the Columbia Mountains in the central portion and the Rocky Mountains in the east. There are a large number of extremely large lakes. The river resources are also vast and provide the province and its neighbors with enormous amounts of electrical energy. If one were to take all the surface fresh water resources of B.C. and combine them into one body of water it would be slightly larger than Lake Ontario in square miles.

Bountiful semiarid valley's are spread among the various mountain ranges and are responsible for the production of many of the food stuffs produced in the province. Around Dawson Creek, in the northeastern corner of the province, one finds evidence of the Great Plains.

The coastal forests are made up of Western Hemlock, Cedar, Spruce and Douglas Fir. The interior regions produce Douglas Fir, Ponderosa Pine, Spruce, and Lodgepole Pine and both regions support the many species of deciduous trees. These forest resources make lumber and pulp and paper making leading industries of British Columbia.

British Columbia

British Columbia is a fisherman's and hunter's paradise. The ocean provides salmon, halibut, cod, numerous bottom fish and shellfish. The fresh waters offer the chance to hook steelhead and several varieties of fat trout. As for mammals, the list is long and impressive. Grizzly and black bear, mountain goat and sheep, moose, elk, cougar, wolves, wolverine, gray whale, Orcas, dolphin, seals, and sea lions, just to name a few. Needless to say hunting and fishing can be quite exciting. The provincial government is quite careful to control both hunting and fishing.

The economy of the province relies greatly on the natural resources. This region is rich in forest, a variety of precious minerals, petroleum, natural gas, coal, hydroelectric power and natural beauty. The provincial government owns almost all the timber lands. A very small portion is in private hands and a smaller portion yet is controlled by the federal government - much different than is the case in the United States where the federal government controls much of the forest.

Greater Vancouver is the commercial and manufacturing center of the province and accounts for almost half of the province's population. Vancouver is good place to do business with the Pacific Rim countries and as such its port facilities are among the busiest on North America's West Coast. Commercial fishing is an important industry. Tourism is a leading industry and film making and fashion clothing are gaining in importance. The strong reliance upon natural resources has caused the governmental and business communities to seek out high-tech and other business enterprises that will broaden the economic base.

The population is heterogeneous, with Aboriginals, Asians, Eastern Europeans, British and Northern Europeans well represented. About fifty percent of the population can trace their ancestry back to the British. The province is also growing with migration being experienced from the eastern provinces of Canada. Most of the population is located in the lower southwestern mainland, Vancouver Island, and the south central portions of the province. The central and northern parts of the British Columbia tend to be more primitive and the communities are generally small, with Prince George being the exception.

Most communities of any size can provide medical services that meet the normal demands of a population. If the medical problem requires specialized treatment then the person will be transported to one of the regional hospitals located in the larger communities.

The provincial government provides funds for the K-12 schools. The local programs are controlled by local school boards but they respond to the standards set by the provincial government. The curriculum is emphasizing mathematics, science, computer skills and international studies along with other basics. Vocational training in knowledge intensive occupations is also receiving much attention. The programs are oriented toward providing a well educated work force.

Communities will use either the RCMP or a municipal police force to provide police protection. Fire protection in the larger cities is provided by paid professional and in smaller communities a small paid staff with volunteers is normal.

Vancouver and Calgary, Alberta are the main continental and international terminals for air transportation. Connector flights from smaller communities are readily available for most of the regions.

The climate varies depending on location. The islands off the West coast experience a marine climate. They are sunny and warm in the summer and it rains in the winter. Snow is not a great problem. This climatic condition is also true for the southern part of the West coast mainland. The northern part of the coast will have cooler summers and somewhat colder winters with more rain and snow. This portion of the coast often feels the full brunt of Pacific storms. It is not protected by the mountains of Vancouver Island or the islands off the coast.

Once one crosses the Coastal Mountains to the interior, the climatic conditions change. On the interior plateau one will experience dryer conditions with an annual rain fall being around 20 inches. The exception to this is in the Kootenay region where the west side of the Rocky Mountains will cause the clouds to lose their moisture. The rainfall here will vary from 15 inches to 100 inches depending on altitude.

British Columbia

The summers for the interior will be pleasantly warm and the winters will be cold. The farther north one goes, the colder one can expect the winters. Of course, as one would expect, the higher the altitude, the colder the weather and the larger the amounts of rain and snow.

There is a section in the south central portion of B.C. called "The Arizona of British Columbia". This is a semiarid region with great lakes and medium size mountains. The summer weather is hot and dry. The winters in the valleys are relatively mild with the mountains experiencing most of the snow and cold weather. This is the place that tourist flock to in the summer to enjoy the lakes and sun. In the winter it draws tourists for skiing.

With the exception of the Greater Vancouver area, real estate prices are quite reasonable when compared to the larger metropolitan communities on the West coast of the United States. Always remember that Canadian prices will be about 30-35% less in U.S. dollars. (Advice for the non-citizen: If one plans on purchasing real estate in B.C. it is strongly suggested that one work with a professional Realtor or an attorney familiar with real estate transaction. If one is planning on retiring in Canada then be sure to consult the Canadian Immigration Service. Canada is like the States in many ways but because it is a separate nation, Canada has its own way of doing things. It is prudent to consult the experts about a matter as serious as retiring in Canada or buying property there.)

Most of the smaller communities have their own unique festivals and celebrations. Almost any day during the summer a person can find a community celebrating music, or art or perhaps some historic episode of significance. Rodeos and festivals of all kinds are popular with the folks of British Columbia. The communities with larger populations and adequate facilities will produce and sponsor symphony orchestras, theatrical production, performances of national and international entertainers and professional sporting events.

British Columbia has a number of ethnic groups and many celebrations are designed to pass on the culture of a particular group. There are any number of museums that have preserved the culture of the Pacific Northwest Indians. If one

British Columbia

is into totem poles and their stories then B.C. is a good place for research.

With the ocean, lakes, rivers and mountains, outdoor recreation is very popular with the people of B.C. and its visitors. One can not help but be impressed with the opportunities to enjoy water activities. Fishing, in the interior, is excellent on the many lakes and rivers. Rafting the rivers is exciting and can match the thrills of almost any rivers in the world.

The Strait of Georgia, the Inside Passage, Queen Charlotte Strait and the Strait of Juan de Fuca provide excellent fishing opportunities. Sailing, motor boating, canoeing and kayaking are enjoyed by thousands. Scuba diving off the east coast of Vancouver Island is felt to be some of the best in the world. Winter, when the water is clearest, is considered the best time for diving activity.

Skiing is another pastime for which B.C. is famous. Whistler Ski Resort, in the western part of the province, is noted as the number one ski resort in North America. It is not alone in providing good ski conditions. More than half of the province is higher than 4,200 feet and so there is plenty of snow. Almost every community has a nearby ski area. There are over 35 ski areas in B.C. Heli-skiing is available in many of the ski areas. One can also expect to find countless opportunities to enjoy cross country skiing, snowshoeing, snowmobiling, ice fishing and other cold weather activities. In the summer the mountainous areas provide vast opportunities for hiking, mountain climbing, and camping.

There are over 225 golf courses in British Columbia. Most of them are located in the southern portion of the province, where the population is located. On Vancouver Island, because of the weather, a person can enjoy golfing year around and that is also true of the mainland around Vancouver. Across the mountains, to the east, the golfing weather will run from April thru October but that doesn't mean that a person can not sneak a game or two in during some good weather in the winter.

The provincial parks and the mountains provide splendid opportunities to enjoy hiking and exploring. Camping is also provided for by the parks. There are a number of guest ranches, fishing camps and resorts that give the "tenderfoot"

British Columbia

a touch of what it's like to be a cowboy/cowgirl, catch a big salmon or enjoy an exciting day on the slopes or the golf course.

If a person has never been to British Columbia this author, without hesitation, recommends one go there before leaving this planet. British Columbia is undoubtedly one of the most inspiring and beautiful places in the Pacific Northwest.

Penticton (32,700 Pop.)

The Indians of the past referred to the Penticton area as "A Place to Live Forever". Indeed it is! It is a pleasant community and is popular with retirees and tourists.

Approaching Penticton from the south on Hwy 97 one notes the "lumpy" appearance of the mountains that border the valley. These are rounded mountains and at their base they afford a large number of residential view sites. The community is located on a flat, relatively narrow, plain and hillsides between two very large and beautiful lakes - Okanagan and Skaha Lake. One can feel the "bigness" of this region by realizing that Okanagan Lake, a natural lake, is 75 miles in length and with Skaha, the total of the two lakes approaches 90 miles.

In a survey conducted by Environment Canada, Penticton was rated the lowest score, 16, out of 100 possible on the Climate Severity Index. A low score indicate a people friendly climate. Other Canadian cities such as Ottawa, Montreal, Edmonton and Calgary didn't fair as well.

The summers are warm and like other semiarid areas, humidity is not a problem. This allows the summers to be very pleasant. With the inviting lakes at its doorstep, Penticton has become a popular resort to many of the people of Canada and the United States.

The winters can be cold but are usually not extremely uncomfortable. The snow in the nearby mountains is great for skiing. The town itself has a mean snowfall of 69 cm or 27 inches. Apex Resort, a popular ski resort in the mountains, is just a short distance from Penticton, consequently many of the skiers seek lodging and entertainment in the town.

In the early 90s, the community growth rate was about 3% per year. Projections for the latter part of the century are pegged at about 2.4% annually.

Penticton's economy revolves around agriculture, tourism, wood products, mining, some manufacturing, and regional services. Apricots, cherries, peaches, pears, prunes, apples and grapes dominate the fruit growing industry of the area. Wines are becoming a big interest in the Okanagan region. The B.C. wine industry has chosen Penticton as the host site of the newly instituted Wine Information Center. The wines that come out of the Okanagan region are gaining fame worldwide.

Three of the largest employers in the valley are a result of the regional service function. The Penticton Regional Hospital, School District 67 and the City of Penticton are responsible for much of the employment in the community.

Another large employer is the tourist industry. There are numerous motels, restaurants and other businesses oriented toward the tourist industry. In B.C. the largest trade and convention center outside of Vancouver exists in Penticton. It has a 443 seat lecture hall and a main ballroom that can seat 3,500 for programs or accommodate 2,400 for meals.

Manufacturing is concerned with wood products, truck trailers, modular and log homes, recreational vehicles, plus speciality food items. Mining is located nearby and the main minerals mined are gold and copper. Price received for the mined minerals is instrumental in determining how much the mines are worked.

Like many other desirable communities, Penticton has a large retirement population. The retiree, with his/her pension, can enhance the economic stability of a community. In Penticton pensions and retirement funds account for over third of the total income from all sources.

Another industry that is starting to grow is the home-based business. It is estimated that 20% of the single family units now have some type of home-based business.

The homes in the town proper are modest, well kept and, for the most part, attractive. There are many "ranch" style homes available which are popular with retirees. The hillsides on both sides of the community provide sites for larger more contemporary homes and many of these have magnificent views of the city, lakes and mountains. Larger pieces of property can be found nearer the mountains and forests.

Summerland is located to the northwest of Penticton. It is situated in the foothills and is an attractive community with many lovely homes. It is near Penticton and acts as a quasi-suburban community.

Housing costs are very reasonable relative to what the prices are in the larger urban areas in the lower mainland. This factor coupled with the desirableness of the community makes Penticton very attractive to those who are looking for a better lifestyle than is afforded by many urban areas.

Good smaller homes can be found at $140,000 and up. Newer and larger homes will range from the mid $200,000s to the upper $300,000s, depending on location. There are some fine homes that have small acreage that will be priced in the $300,000s. (All prices are Canadian.)

The educational scene is equipped with a school district that consistently turns out graduates that score higher than average on the provincial examinations. The enrollment is 7,900 which allows a staffing size capable of delivering a comprehensive curriculum.

In addition to the K-12 program, Penticton has an extension campus from Okanagan University College. This campus provides for the first two years of an university degree program, a high school completion program, an adult basic education program and a number of other programs designed to answer the community's adult education needs and desires.

The Penticton Regional Hospital is a 307 bed regional facility and it provides a comprehensive program. Vancouver's hospitals augment the services of the hospital by taking patients who need highly specialized treatment, like open-heart or neurological surgeries.

Police and fire protection services are provided by paid professionals. The police force is staffed with RCMP officers. Fire personnel also respond to emergency and medical calls. There is a 911 system in the community.

The airport is at the edge of the town. Commuter flights to Calgary or Vancouver for continental or international flights are available. The runway is paved and approaches 6,000 feet and there is also a navigational system available.

British Columbia

The community has several theater groups, a symphony, light opera, the Progress Theater Company Society, art galleries, museums, a 400 seat performing arts theater, a 275 seat community theater, a trade and convention center, an arena and a curling rink. Needless to say this community has many exciting opportunities for cultural and entertainment pursuits.

Celebrations, festivals and other unique community activities feature: the Peach Festival, the Ironman Triathlon with over 1,800 athletes competing, the Square Dancing Jamboree, and a popular Wine Festival. Also supported by the locals and tourists is a large game farm south of the city. The Art Gallery of the South Okanagan is a nonprofit organization and presents contemporary, historical, national and international exhibits. The Leir House Cultural Center provides studio space for artist and musicians plus meeting areas for workshops and seminars. The Okanagan Summer School for the Arts is an annual affair in July dedicated to encouraging fine arts and music. The list of activities that are available, for a city Penticton's size, is quite impressive and perhaps another reason for its attractiveness for the urban refugee.

The list of recreational activities is just as extensive. Apex Mountain Resort provides great downhill skiing and it is only 30 minutes from downtown. The lakes have house boating opportunities. The Skaha Bluffs are available for rock climbing. Biking and hiking along the old road bed of the Kettle Valley Railway is appealing to many. Golf anyone? There are a number golf courses within easy commute and many years people play golf year around. In addition to the above, a person can take up mountain climbing, parasailing, hang gliding, sky diving, boating, fishing, hunting, windsurfing and if that is not enough, how about hockey or curling? If one is into total fitness then they might want to enter the Ironman Triathlon.

Just where is Penticton? It is located 221 miles north of Spokane, 424 miles west of Calgary, 313 miles northeast of Seattle and 244 miles east of Vancouver.

Summary: Penticton is a "gem" of a community. The climate, its natural environment, good services, reasonable housing, cultural, entertainment and recreational opportunities make

British Columbia

Penticton a very attractive city for the retiree and the urban refugee who is seeking a simpler and perhaps more fulfilling lifestyle.

Kelowna (92,000 Pop.)

Uplake from Penticton is the exciting community of Kelowna. This community, if one is coming from the south, is reached via a floating bridge that crosses Okanagan Lake. The lake narrows at this point and the towns of Westbank and Kelowna occupy the hills and narrow valley that surrounds each side of the lake. Kelowna presents one with favorable living conditions, a temperate climate and the natural beauty of the lake and the hillsides and mountains.

This community is one of the largest commercial centers in the Okanagan region. It has some very fine residential sections that are graced with inspiring views of the valley and the lake. It is and has been, one of the faster growing communities in British Columbia. Westbank, which is west and across the lake from Kelowna, is primarily a residential community with homes perched high on hillsides.

Downtown Kelowna is a busy place and exemplifies the commercial aspects of the community. The primary drivers of the economy are agriculture, forestry and wood products, truck vehicle manufacturing, tourism and regional services. High-tech is gaining a strong foothold and it is hoped to become a major influence in the near future.

A newer three bedroom/two bath home price will start in the $170,000s and go up. There are a number of splendid development on golf courses, with lake front or with stunning views. Small lakefront lots can be found for $100,000 plus. Large homes with city and or lake view can be found in the $400,000 range and then there are the magnificent homes on the lake or with small acreage that will cost from $500,000 up. (All prices are Canadian) The use of stucco and tile roofs, similar to architectural styles found in the southwestern U.S., is popular.

A new master plan development is in progress. It is called Kettle Valley and is designed to bring folks back into model neighborhoods. It will have the garages accessible via

British Columbia

back lanes (alleys). The homes will have front porches and sidewalks. Brick exteriors are standard and stucco is not allowed. There will be over 1000 homes when completed. The development will overlook the city lights, wineries and sparkling Okanagan Lake. The development will have shopping within walking distance. (Such a place should appeal to those looking for a simpler lifestyle and who see value in the early 20th century neighborhood concept.)

School District 23 is a large district. Its enrollment is over 22,000 pupils. A district this large can support a comprehensive educational program.

Kelowna is also the home of Okanagan University College. This is a two and four-year degree granting institution. It provides five campus throughout the Okanagan region and it serves 11,000 students.

Kelowna General hospital is a 685 bed facility and is capable of providing comprehensive medical services to the region. In 1998 the hospital will open a new cancer center. Fire and police protection is provided by paid professions. The community has a 911 system.

The airport is capable of handling jet aircraft. It provides connecting flights to Calgary and Vancouver for longer continental and international flights.

Kelowna supports a symphony, a professional theater company and a number of fine art galleries and museums. Some of the festivals supported by the community are: the Kelowna Jazz Festival, the Mozart Festival, the Okanagan Wine Festival, the Folk Fest, lectures series, boat and car shows, rodeos, hydroplane races and the Kelowna Regatta and Mardi Gras. Tourism promotes night life and many fine dining opportunities.

Recreationally Kelowna has a lot to offer. There are three downhill ski resorts within one hour. Big White, a ski resort to the east, has recently enhanced its facilities with a 4.5 million dollar investment. This area is noted for its dry snow and an impressive abundance of the "white stuff". Most of the snow falls in the mountains and is not considered a big problem in the valley. Where there is downhill one always finds opportunities to enjoy cross country skiing, snowshoeing and snowmobiling.

British Columbia

Of course, with the mountains, there are opportunities for camping, hiking, backpacking, fishing, horseback riding and hunting. The lake allows for a multitude of activities: parasailing, house boating, sailing, water skiing, swimming, fishing and windsurfing. The community supports triathlons and a Sea to Sky Race which involves teams participating in skiing, running and canoeing.

The climate is semiarid with loads of sunshine and only an average of 13 inches of precipitation annually. The summers are hot and just right for some fun on the beautiful lake and at the many golf courses available. There are 10 golf courses within 30 minutes of Kelowna. A number of the courses have been recognized by Golf Digest as 4 star facilities. The winters are mild in the valley but within easy reach of snow country and its excitement.

Calgary is 325 miles to the east. Vancouver is 280 miles to the west and Seattle 302 miles. Spokane, to the south, is 245 miles.

Summary: Kelowna possesses the excitement of a town that is the industrial and commercial center for a large geographical region. It has the services and retail outlets that many have come to depend on in their everyday life. The economy is stable and well diversified.

Housing is reasonable both from the perspective of a State-side person and a urban dweller from Canada. The community services are good and opportunities to participate in the cultural and recreational activities are plentiful.

The climate is ideal for a four season environment and the natural environment is beautiful and quite inviting.

All in all, Kelowna is an inviting place and deserves closer scrutiny from someone interested in a less stressful environment with all the services of a larger urban area.

British Columbia

Kamloops (80,000 Pop.)

Kamloops is a medium size city that has a lot to offer. It is located at the junction of the North and South Thompson rivers which go on to make up the larger Thompson River which finally ends up joining the Fraser River. This is a region that has hundreds of lakes which make fishing one of the major interests. This community is known as Tournament Capital of British Columbia and plays host to a number of sporting tournaments.

The downtown section of the city is located in the valley floor next to the beautiful Thompson River. There are a number of smaller communities that are on the north side of the river, south and to the east of Kamloops proper. For all intents and purposes they go to make up greater Kamloops. In the early half of the nineties Kamloops grew quite rapidly, but the growth has slowed somewhat in recent years. Kamloops is popular with retirees.

The hillsides are clustered with a number of residential developments. The views from many of the residences are magnificent. Not only does Kamloops have several rivers flowing through the community but it also has some rugged mountains nearby that adds to the panoramic nature of the views.

The climate causes hot dry summers and cold snowy winters. The growing season averages 150 days a year.

The economy is one of the most diversified outside British Columbia's lower mainland. It's economy is based around forest and wood products, agriculture, mining, governmental services, and tourism. Raising cattle is important in this region. There are over 150 ranches nearby and besides the animals, production of forage crops take up a rancher's time.

Something unique to this region is the production of ginseng. This crop was introduced a short while back and has caught on. A processing plant was completed recently. It is predicted by the B.C. Ministry of Agriculture that ginseng will be the biggest cash crop of British Columbia in the near future.

British Columbia

Kamloops Reserve (Reservation), across the river from downtown Kamloops, has an industrial park and is looking to develop a resort in the near future. Also located in Kamloops is the headquarters of the B.C. Lottery. Retirees and governmental services provide considerable stability to Kamloops economy. Kamloops is located at the junction of three major highways and two railroad.

A three bedroom/two bath home can be found in the $140,000 range. Homes on small acreage will cost in the neighborhood of $150,000s and up. Newer executive homes will cost in the high $100,000s and up. View executive homes will range from the mid $200,000s and up. (The prices are Canadian.) More modest housing can be found in some of the smaller surrounding communities.

The public school system is a large district with an enrollment of 17,400 pupils. This enrollment provides a school district capable of maintaining a comprehensive curricular program for its pupils. The University College of the Cariboo (Yes, the spelling is correct) is a 4 year degree granting university with a student body over 7,500.

The Royal Inland Hospital provides acute care for the region and for highly specialized services the hospitals in Vancouver are available. The police protection is provide by the RCMP and fire protection by professional firefighters. 911 is available. The Kamloops airport provides commuter services to Calgary and Vancouver for continental and international flights.

Kamloops supports professional theater, a symphony orchestra, art galleries and a museum. The Western Canadian Theater Company performs in the 730 seat Sagebrush Theater and Pavilion Theater. The Kamloops Riverside Coliseum is home to the Western Hockey League's Kamloops Blazers. This is a team that the community is very proud of and supports strongly. Since this is cattle country some fine rodeos are put on annually. The heritage of the community is on display at the wonderful Kamloops Powwow. This three day affair presents hundreds of performers. One must not forget the Kamloops Wildlife Park if they are interested in native and exotic animals.

British Columbia

Like many other communities in this region there are any number of recreational activities of which to partake. Several of the more unique activities to this community are the Championship Dragon Boat Races, cattle drives where "tenderfoots" can tag along, and horse racing at Sagebrush Downs. Kamloops, to mention a few other activities, also has downhill skiing at Suns Peaks Resort, cross country skiing, snowmobiling, curling, hockey, hunting, fishing, hiking, boating, water skiing, windsurfing and lots of golfing opportunities. Whitewater rafting is available on the Thompson, Clearwater and Chilliwack rivers.

Kamloops is part of the high interior plateau. It is 213 miles from Vancouver, 371 miles from Calgary and 278 miles from Seattle. Spokane is 342 miles to the south.

Summary: Kamloops, with its present day vitality and pioneer heritage, is a city that has a lot going for it. The economy is diversified, housing is reasonable, community services are good, culturally and recreationally there is something for everyone. It definitely has four seasons with extremes in the summer and the winter. This is a community for the adventuresome and the hardy. If one is interested in sports it is a community that could accommodate those needs. The mountains, lakes, rivers and the forest all go to bring one an exciting environment in which to live.

Whistler (7,500 Pop.)

Whistler is a thriving, exciting, affluent resort-type community coupled with the calm, rejuvenating atmosphere of a beautiful alpine valley. There are countless opportunities to keep a young family or a retired couple wholesomely busy. During its short history it has been more attractive to the younger clientele but this is changing and the retirees and permanent residents are starting to settle in the community.

Being a resort community, its first focus has been in developing a community that is attractive to tourists who want to enjoy winter and summer sporting activities. It is approaching the "build-out" parameters issued when it was designated as a resort municipality and now the community leaders are

British Columbia

turning their attention to community services that will serve the permanent residents.

Whistler is nestled in among the beautiful and inspiring Coastal Range mountains of Canada. It has considerable snow in the winter and is a premier ski area. As stated before, Whistler has the distinction of being recognized as the number one ski resort in North America.

Not only does the winter snow bring visitors who like to ski but the summer sunshine brings visitors who like to play golf. Whistler has three very challenging golf courses, designed by top professionals.

The community will annually serve as a playground for over 650,000 winter visitors and 550,000 summer visitors. This is definitely a four season resort with mountains, rivers and crystal clear lakes. These natural amenities provide opportunities for countless outdoor activities.

The economy of the area is driven by tourism and the services required by a community. Retailing and other resort-type services keep the labor force employed. Constructions has been, and for the near future, will continue to be a major driver in the community. Because the village is approaching "build-out", commercial construction will diminish and future construction will be more concerned with the needs of the local people, i.e., schools, public safety complex, homes, churches. This slow-down in construction will slow the economy and the leaders of the community are on the lookout for businesses and industries that will flourish in a resort/retirement community.

The economic impact of Whistler on the surrounding areas is that of a magnet that draws people to the region. With its growth restrictions, the other nearby communities are expected to grow as an alternative for housing and services for visitors or permanent residents.

As one would expect properties are increasing in value. Fine single family residences can be found in the $500,000 range and attractive condos are available from the mid $100,000s and up. (Remember, these are Canadian prices.) Time shares are available and are reasonable. Resort Condominiums International (RCI) gives Whistler its highest rating.

British Columbia

This is a community where the housing is very appealing to a visitor as well as to someone who wants to make it a permanent situation. The best way to describe the building sites for single family homes is to say they have mountains all around and are white and silent in the winter and green and scented in the springs, summers and falls.

Whistler has a small school district that is organized K-7 and 8-12. Its enrollment is less than 1,000. There is a health care center that can handle most of the needs of the community. For hospitalization the hospital at Squamish is used. If the case needs highly specialized services the Vancouver hospitals are called upon.

Police protection is provided by the RCMP and fire protection is provided by paid professionals. The fire personnel are trained in EMT techniques. There is a 911 system and the Emergency Health Service personnel respond to emergency calls with back-up provided by fire personnel.

Whistler doesn't have a hard runway but float planes land in nearby Green Lake. Pemberton, a nearby community, has an airport that can receive and service small jets. Vancouver airport provides services for continental and international flights.

Whistler exists for one reason and that is to provide recreational opportunities. It is noted for its skiing. The longest ski run at Blackcomb/Whistler is over 11km (7 miles). The resort has the most up-to-date equipment and runs that fit all skill levels. It is a place where one might find the World Cup races one week and the World Ski and Snowboard Festival the next. After a hard day on the slopes there are any number of establishments where a person can relax and have a good Canadian beverage.

The golf courses at Whistler were designed by world renown course architects and golfers. First, there is Chateau Whistler Golf Club designed by Robert Trent Jones Jr.. There is a course designed by Jack Nicklaus called Nicklaus North at Whistler. The third course is called Whistler Golf Club and it was designed by Arnold Palmer. These courses are all championship courses and a challenge to even pros. The courses in the nearby communities are also challenging.

British Columbia

One will also find opportunities to snowshoe, cross country ski, snowmobile, ice fish, play hockey, ice skate, hike, mountain bike, hang glide, boat and swim. If shopping is important, the retailers in the Village will be glad to accommodate.

Now you say where is this wonderful place called Whistler? If one takes Hwy 99 north from Vancouver in about 2 hours, depending on the weather and traffic, one should arrive at Whistler. Whistler is about a 4-5 hours from Seattle.

Summary: Whistler is an upscale resort community but it can and probably will take on a more permanent atmosphere as the "build-out" is reached. The community is moving away from its narrow focus on tourist needs and broadening its operations to include services needed to serve a more permanent community. Like most resort communities real estate is relatively expensive. The community is interested in expanding its economic base.

This is a community of unmatched beauty. It is a community that has a refreshing climate and loads of things to do. It snows in the winter and is delightfully warm in the summer. It is not so isolated that a quick trip to the city is impossible. It is a young, fun, contemporary community.

The community services are good and getting better. Medical care is sufficient for most cases. If specialized medical services are needed they are available but not locally. Police and fire protection is provided by professionals. The schools are small but will grow. Transportation to the community is usually by car, and rail transportation is available. Pemberton can provide connector air service. To sum it up, Whistler is an exciting place or it can be a calm and relaxing place to live - depending on one's lifestyle choice. It is certainly worthy of serious investigation.

British Columbia

Victoria (76,000 Pop.)*

At the southern end of Vancouver Island is Victoria. It is the capital of British Columbia and is the nearest thing to an English community one will find in the Pacific Northwest. This is a beautiful city with its gardens, colorful English shops, and busy harbor full of boats of every description. This city is noted for its flowers, in fact, each year they go so far as to have an annual flower count. Tea rooms abound and visitors love to have tea in the old, but very impressive, Empress Hotel. Victoria is a favorite with tourist who want a touch of "Old England".

As the capital of the province, Victoria's economy is quite reliant upon the provincial government's operation. Recently, the government, like so many large organizations, has been "downsizing". This has produced glut in the commercial office space—something for an entrepreneur to take note of. Like all communities Victoria is always on the lookout for ways to diversify it's economy. Greater Victoria serves as a commercial and business center for much of the Vancouver Island population.

There is considerable reliance upon tourism in this community. Tourists come from the States and other parts of Canada to get a taste of British culture and products.

Because of it's favorable climate and beautiful surrounding, this city and its surrounding communities have become popular with retirees. This group adds significantly to the economic stability of the region.

Real estate in this part of the island is more expensive than "up island". Many of the homes in Victoria are older than those found in "up island" cities. These homes appear to be of the early and mid 20th century style. Nicer homes of this type will range in cost from the low $200,000 to the low $300,000.

Large executive homes, some with views, will cost from $300,000 and up. A drive along the ocean front will present some very beautiful estate-like properties. One is reminded,

---

Greater Victoria is composed of four core municipalities, Victoria, Saanich, Esquimalt and Oak Bay. The total population these communities is approximately 215,000.

British Columbia

on this drive, of a similar drive on the island of Oahu when viewing some of that island's finer homes. The homes on the hillside with their panoramic views are also gorgeous. Prices for these stately homes with ocean frontage or fantastic views will range from the mid $400,000 up—way up in a number of cases.

There are three school districts that serve greater Victoria. The two smaller district enroll about 8,000 to 9,000. Victoria has the largest district which enrolls 22,600 pupils. Districts this size are capable of providing a comprehensive curriculum for it pupils.

The University of Victoria is located in the community and it serves almost 15,000 part-time and full-time students. It provides both undergraduate and graduate programs. Camosun College is also located here and it provides academic and vocation/technical programs. There is a small military college call Royal Roads Military College.

The hospital services of greater Victoria are provided by four hospitals. These hospitals are capable of maintaining a comprehensive medical program which not only serves the Victoria area but much of the Island.

Victoria International Airport has 60 scheduled flights daily to the mainland. Vancouver International provides continental and international flight services. There are a number of float plane flights that will take a passenger to a far off lake or distant harbor on the fascinating and inspiring coast of B.C. or Vancouver Island.

Police protection is handled by professionals. Some communities have a municipal police force while other communities are protected by the RCMP - it is a matter of local choice. Fire protection is provided by paid professionals. A 911 system is available.

Victoria provides a great menu of cultural and entertainment opportunities. The Victoria Symphony is outstanding. There are a number of professional and amateur theater and dance companies. The city also has opera. For the art lover the city supports 23 art galleries and several grand museums. The architecture is also very interesting.

Afternoon tea in Victoria is an art form and a very pleasing experience, even for the most "macho" of men. For the

British Columbia

children there is a petting farm and lots of parks. One of the most famous features of the city is its many public and private gardens.

The festival scene is graced with band and jazz programs. There is the Symphony Splash where, in the evening, the orchestra plays from a barge in the harbor and fireworks light up the sky. Folks come from all over to enjoy this musical treat. The garden tours are breathtaking. Illustrative of the festivals that abound are: the Strawberry Festival, the Shakespeare Festival, Classic Boat Festival, and the Classic Canadian Beer Festival. This is a city that can keep a person busy with some very fine cultural and entertainment programs.

As for spectator sports the city provides a stadium, 2 arenas, a car track, horse track, indoor pools, ice arenas, curling rinks, tennis courts, play fields, fitness clubs, yacht clubs, marinas and countless parks. Hockey, soccer and softball programs for the young and the old are available. They have a rodeo and host the Highland Games. In January, if one becomes bored with the mundane, they can always join in the Polar Bear Swim—brrrr. The people of Victoria also enjoy their marathons and triathlons.

Golf should get some special mention. The weather is very mild and golf can be pursued year around. There are eight 18 hole courses and seven 9 hole courses, including the prestigious Royal Oak and Uplands Gold courses.

Boating and water sports are also big in this part of the world. There are sailing races, including the Swiftsure and Vic-Maui Races. There are also trips among the San Juan and the Gulf islands, whale watching, wind surfing, rowing, fishing and scuba diving. Heritage adds some sports that normally don't get much attention in the States, like lawn bowling and cricket.

In the winter one can add skiing to all the sports and physical activities mentioned above. If one gets bored or can't find something to their taste than perhaps a hike in the mountains, forest or sea shore or bungy jumping near Nanaimo might satisfy them. Frequenting the wonderful libraries or bookstores that abound might also do the trick. When all else fails a person can always go shopping—its great!

British Columbia

One must take some form of water or air transportation to get to Victoria from the mainland. This is one of the good things about living in or visiting Vancouver Island. The ferry trip is absolutely inspiring as the ferry moves effortlessly across the water and among beautiful islands.

Vancouver by ferry and car is about a 2 hour trip. Seattle can be reached by taking the ferry from Tsawwassen, Anacortes, or the "Black Ball" ferry to Port Angeles, and then driving the rest of the way. The total trip will take 4 to 5 hours depending on the traffic and or weather. If quick passage is necessary then air transportation, either by float plane or jet is always available. Nanaimo, via a good road, is 68 miles to the north.

Summary: Victoria is a fabulous place to visit and live. There are a number of people leaving the lower mainland to establish themselves on Vancouver Island and Victoria is one of the favored places.

The city is fascinating with its 'British' heritage, beautiful harbor and seashore. The community services are good. There are ample opportunities to take part in cultural and sporting activities. The people are very friendly.

The economy is greatly dependent on commerce, provincial governmental operations and tourism. It has several institutions of higher learning and good police and fire protection. Medical services are readily available and comprehensive. Transportation to and from the island takes time so don't be in a rush. The weather is mild with the summers being very pleasant . The winters are not overly cold and snow is an infrequent visitor. Rainfall is less than Seattle, Chicago, New York and significantly less than most of the East, Southeast and Midwest United States.

This city is charming and appeals to almost everyone. If one is looking for a very nice community with lots to do, then Victoria should get some attention. Even if one decides not to live there, a visit will be a exhilarating experience. Don't forget to have afternoon tea at the Empress or some cozy little tea room - you won't regret it.

Nanaimo (72,000 Pop.)

This is a city about one-third of the way up Vancouver Island and across from Horseshoe Bay on the mainland. The commercial part of town is a mix of the old and new. This is a community that has a healthy hustle bustle to it. It is becoming very popular with mainlanders who are searching for a less hectic lifestyle and a beautiful place to live.

Nanaimo is an excellent home base for visiting other parts of Vancouver Island. It is close to the West coast with its more primitive environment, the north and great fishing, and not too far from Victoria.

The economy thrives on forest and wood products, tourism, government services, transportation services/supplies, and high-tech. The work force is well educated. There are many small businesses and the community is looking for more. Nanaimo provides an all purpose port facility which is important to Nanaimo and the rest of upper Vancouver Island. The largest employers are the school district, the hospital, the college and Harmac Pac Ltd.—a kraft pulp facility. The economy is becoming less dependent on natural resources and moving toward a more diversified economy.

A three bedroom/two bath home will start in the mid $100,000s and up. A nice home with a view will be priced in the mid $200,000s and up. There are a number of homes with ocean view available in the $200,000 and up. Ocean view lots are priced at $50,000 and up. The north end of the community is experiencing considerable growth. Real estate prices went up during the early 90s but have softened the last few years. Nanaimo is popular with retirees and real estate prices are part of the reason. (These are Canadian prices)

Nanaimo has a large hospital. Nanaimo Regional General is capable of providing a comprehensive medical program for the city and surrounding communities. The service of the hospital are supported by hospitals in Victoria and Vancouver.

School District 68 serves Nanaimo and the surrounding communities. The enrollment is 14,000 pupils and at this size a comprehensive program can be provided. Malaspina University College is the degree granting institution located in the community It has an enrollment of 3,500 full time students and 11,000 in extension programs.

The police force is manned by RCMP officers and fire protection is provided by professionals. 911 is available. Flight connector service is available to Vancouver International from the airport serving Nanaimo. The ferry from the mainland comes from Horseshoe Bay, which is just north of Vancouver. Tsawwassen which is south of Vancouver also has ferry service to Nanaimo.

Nanaimo has a performing arts center capable of seating 800. This is the 61 million dollar Harborfront Center Theater. Nanaimo supports a number of theater groups such as the Nanaimo Festival Theater Group and the Yellow Drama Group. The community has its own symphony and the Vancouver Island Symphony also performs. There are any number of groups that present ethnic dances and music, e.g., the German Club Choir, Highland Dancer, Indian Drummers, Ukrainian Dancers and the Bastion City Cloggers. There are art galleries and the Nanaimo District Museum presents the history of the area and the Coast Salish Indians.

Some of the celebrations include Empire Days, the Marine Festival with its crazy Bathtub Race, the Fringe Festival which encourages experimental and undiscovered entertainment and the Jazz and Dixieland Festival.

Golfing is popular in this area. There are 19 golf courses within one hour of Nanaimo and golf can be played almost year around.

Being so near the sea, fishing is readily available. Salmon, cod, red snapper, halibut are the most common fish caught. There are a number of boats with skippers who know where the "big ones" hang out. One of the "locals" described the summer as a time when life is slow and easy. It is a time when thoughts turn to boating, fishing, and other enjoyable past times.

Scuba diving is some of the best in the world. It is said that the Strait and Gulf Islands vicinity is second only to the Red Sea for scuba diving. There are 300 species of sea life and a large number of sunken ships to explore. The water is very clean which make for an excellent diving environment.

If one likes real thrills then there is bungy jumping from a 140 foot high bridge. It is the only legal bridge jump in North America. This sport draws over 50,000 spectators a year and even some jumps.

Skiing is available at Mt. Washington and on the mainland at Whistler. The island is ideal for exploring the forest, mountains and seashore. This involves hiking, camping, boating, flying and off-roading. Nanaimo has a number of lakes for recreation and the city maintains 2,700 acres of park land. Softball and hockey are the favorite sports in the community but that doesn't mean the other sports such as soccer, tennis, and basketball are ignored.

The weather is moderate year around. It rarely gets too hot or too cold. There is lots of sun and the best months are June through September. In the winter it rains on the average of 44 inches and snow can be expected in the winter but it doesn't stay long.

Nanaimo is 68 miles from Victoria and 13 miles from Vancouver. The trip to Vancouver, although not far in miles, take about 2 hours because of the ferry crossing. Seattle is about 130 miles south and requires a ferry ride and a 2 to 3 hour drive.

Summary: Nanaimo was described to this writer as a "safe and gentle place to live." Mainlanders are migrating to this town with the strange name.

Its reliance on natural resources is diminishing and the community is interested in bringing in high-tech and service industries. The economy is diversified and becoming more so with each year. The city has good medical, school and civil services. Real estate prices are reasonable.

There is a great deal to do in this community. The cultural and entertainment opportunities are considerable. The natural environment affords a person some rare opportunities to view sea life as well as that of mountains and forest.

British Columbia

This is a very pleasant community that has warm and sunny summers and rainy winters but neither season is extreme. It is most definitely worth a ferry ride which will introduce you to some of the most beautiful scenery and finest people in the world. Who knows, this might just be the place for which you are looking.

Some Advice

If one is considering relocation to one of the communities discussed, then it is suggested they visit the community. A person might also want to consider some of the following:

> Interview the people at the Chamber of Commerce and several real estate offices. These people are generally well informed about the community and/or know of another person who is familiar with the community.
>
> Subscribe to the local newspaper.
>
> Secure a map of the surrounding region. Talk with folks from the city government to find out what the plans are for expansion and where the community is experiencing problems, e.g., water, sewer, streets.
>
> Talk to those who are new to the community to see what they have to say.
>
> Check the weather for the four seasons - summers can be great and winters can be tough.
>
> Check-out where people shop and what they do for recreation and entertainment.
>
> Have a visit with the school district superintendent.
>
> Visit the police department, the fire department and the medical facilities to find out what services they provide.

Another practical suggestion is to visit the community on a vacation. This gives a person the opportunity to get a "feel" for the community. If this is the place, consider renting before buying. If looking for a house or some land to buy, be

Some Advice

sure to secure the services of a Realtor. Realtors know the area and they know the real estate laws and procedures in their local community.

Most of the small communities have difficulty employing their present citizens. Therefore, be cautioned not to go to small communities if employment is a critical issue. Several of the larger communities appeared to have jobs available for skilled workers. In any event, make sure that the local employment scene is explored.

If a person has a business, the communities will welcome you with open arms. Large enterprises that will put the small "mom and pop" stores out of business, sometime run into resistance. Light industry, which is environmentally clean, is usually welcome in most communities.

People who remember they are the "new kids" on the block and try to fit in, will get along very well in their new community. The people in the Pacific Northwest are, for the most part, friendly and readily accept newcomers who don't try to change them or the way they have been doing things.

Many people ask what communities I found most appealing. Well, here are my favorites and the main reasons I choose them:

    Wenatchee and Walla Walla, Washington
    Bend/Sisters/Redmond, Ashland/Medford and Eugene, Oregon
    Boise and Coeur d'Alene, Idaho
    Bozeman and Missoula, Montana
    Victoria and Kelowna, British Columbia

What made me pick these communities?

    1. They are all medium size or larger communities. I've spent most of my life in medium size cities and to go to a very small rural area would probably be too much of a change for me at this point in life.

    2. They all have comprehensive medical facilities. This is important to a person who has had three by-pass operations.

    3. They all have an institution of higher learning. Universities and colleges add greatly to the intellectual and cultural environment of a community.

Some Advice

4. With the exception of Eugene, they all have lots of sun.
I like sun and four distinct seasons. Eugene has a mild climate with fairly wet winters but its cultural and recreational environments offset the moisture.

In closing, I hope the information presented in this book will be of value to the reader. If you are a stranger to the Pacific Northwest, please come and visit, perhaps you will decide to stay.

I'd like to leave you with this thought. When I try to describe the beauty and grandeur of the Pacific Northwest I am reminded of the visitor who was on a hike in the mountains of Washington. It was one of those chilly mountain nights. He was sitting by the campfire, sipping his hot cup of coffee, and reflecting on the beauty of the Cascades, their stillness, and the dazzling display of the star-filled heavens. It was observed by his companions that he had been silent for a long time. Then, just barely above the crackle of the fire, he was heard to whisper to himself, "This surely is the place where the Lord came to rest on the seventh day."

Order Form

To order additional copies of:

Finding Your Own Eden
There's a Place for You in the Pacific Northwest

please send $14.95 plus $2.50
Shipping & Handling,
Washington residents please include 8.6% sales tax. Make check or money order payable to:

Hanna Enterprises
11410 N.E. 124th St. Ste.491
Kirkland, WA 98034

_____Copies @ $14.95 ea._____
$2.50 Shipping & Handling_____
Washington State residents add 8.6%_____
Total enclosed_____

Name_____
Address_____
City, State, Zip_____

Name_____
Address_____
City, State, Zip_____

Name_____
Address_____
City, State, Zip_____

Please list on a separate sheet
additional addresses where copies are to be sent.